Something Amazing

Something Amazing

Cape Wrath to Cape Horn
by way of Peru

Rebecca Ridgway

Hodder & Stoughton
LONDON SYDNEY AUCKLAND

British Library Cataloguing in Publication Data

Ridgway, Rebecca
  Something Amazing
  I. Title
941.085092

ISBN 0-340-57480-1

Published by Hodder and Stoughton,
a division of Hodder and Stoughton Ltd,
Mill Road, Dunton Green, Sevenoaks, Kent TN13 2YA.
Editorial Office: 47 Bedford Square, London WC1B 3DP.

Photoset by Rowland Phototypesetting Ltd,
Bury St Edmunds, Suffolk

Printed in Great Britain by
St Edmundsbury Press Ltd, Bury St Edmunds, Suffolk

To
my mother and father,
Justin and Nigel
for their love,
help and inspiration.

Acknowledgements for the Cape Horn Expedition

Dad, thanks for believing in me and putting up with my rattiness.

With special thanks to my father, John Ridgway (*Rockwater 2*), without whose time, hard work and relentless tenacity, none of us would have had the opportunity to canoe round Cape Horn.

Mum and Justin for continual support, encouragement and with whom I could share my fears.

Gran for her love and unending determination to stop me doing these sort of things.

Reg for accepting numerous last-minute parcels, letting Dad and me cover your flat with kit, and putting us up so many times.

Lance and Ada for their unfailing security, high standards and love.

Marrack Goulding (Uncle Mig), Under-Secretary General for the UN Peacekeeping Forces, for helping to smooth the "official" route.

To the whole team, without whom the trip would not have been so successful and enjoyable.

On the water:

Nigel (*Rockwater 3*) for teaching me, dragging me out of the sea on numerous occasions, believing I could do it and always being there, keeping a watchful eye.

JW (*Rockwater 5*) for all the hours of training at Ardmore, reassurance, always being there when conditions got worse – and "bits and bobs".

Aled (*Rockwater 4*) for always laughing at my worried expressions, all the tips and hard work on the kayaks.

Chris (*Rockwater 6*) for lightheartedness and fun.

Boycie (*Rockwater 6*) for epic drive and reporting.

Hoppy (*Rockwater 7*) for exciting moments during winter training and stickier work.

Igor (*Rockwater 7*) for being a great friend, adding Latin flavour and fun, and for "the birds above me sing a song – a gentle sweet refrain."

On board *Compass Rose*:

Jack Tolson for filming it all for posterity and for knowledge of the sea area.

Nigel Tedeschi for excellent satellite communications.

Richard Morris Adams for so many things – the one who kept us all together, acted as quartermaster, expedition artist, masseur, baker, interviewer, press adviser, commentator for Cape Horn helicopters, but most of all for his optimism, cheerfulness and being such a good friend to Dad.

The Chilean crew of *Compass Rose* for their excitement and their will for us all to succeed.

Conrado Alvarez, skipper, for his knowledge and skill in handling *Compass Rose*, as well as open emotion.

Lucho, mate and engineer, for his skill and cheerfulness.

Pato, cook, for miraculous meals and entertainment.

Thanks to Alex Fairweather at Ardmore for the suppleness training.

Dr Craddock, our local doctor, for medical advice and injections.

Thanks to all those at Anglesey Sea and Surf Centre for always making us welcome:

Joni for hospitality and support.

Joan for many telephone messages between JR and Nigel.

Snowy for good breakfasts to see us through many wet days.

Mike Webb for hours of work on the kayaks.

Mike for my very wet introduction to surfing.

Roger and Penny for numerous stitches at the Mouse Loft.

Judy and Romi for their help wrapping and packing food into the crate.

Thanks to those in Chile who got things moving via long-distance telephone calls and faxes: Cathy and Hugh MacLeay; Nick Asheshov for finding Helen Fell; Helen and Pedro Fell for the charter of *Compass Rose*, and all those at Arka Patagonia.

Thanks to the Chilean Marines at Punta Arenas, especially Lieutenant Eduardo.

Thanks to the Chilean Navy for their hire of the helicopter and

Acknowledgements

Castor, and especially to Commander Swett at Puerto Williams. And for the great hospitality that was shown to us by those at Porto Toro, and the radio operators at Cape Ross and Cape Horn.

All those at Hostal Roca in Punta Arenas; Mario and family at the Hostal Ona Shaga in Puerto Williams.

Thanks for letting us realise our dream in Chilean waters: Admiral Jorge Martinez Busch, Commander-in-Chief, Chilean Navy; Ambassador Juan Somavia, Chilean Mission UN; Rear Admiral Octavio Bolelli Luna, Chief of Naval Mission, London; Captain Victor Wilson, Assistant Naval Attaché, London.

Very special thanks to David Dey, Director, British Telecom for believing in us and backing the trip. For BT support, Keith Clark, Bill Whyte, Phil Brierly, Edward Scott, Tom Rowbotham, David Barzilay and Steve Woolhouse.

Norman "Get your fat ass down there, John" Chambers, Jan Veldwick and Scott Lyons at Rockwater.

Steve Hinton and Clive Jelley at Rail Freight Services; Mike Hay and Alison Aitken at Survival Anglia; Bill Taylor and Nick Pollard at ITN *News at Ten*; Will Elsworth-Jones and Nick Crane at the *Weekend Telegraph*; Brian Cunningham, Howard Ford and Steve Walker at IBM on whose lap-top this book has been written; John Hunt at Rolex; Phil McGuinness at Benjamin Ackerley Shipping; Peter Buchanan at the Met Office, Aberdeen; Cathy Derrick at *Blue Peter*; Wil Aaran at S4C Hel Straeon; Michael White at LO-KATA Ltd; Peta Stuart-Hunt for GARMIN GPS 100 at Willoughby Stewart Associates.

With special thanks for their time and support with equipment and food: Chris Hawkesworth – Wild Water/Mont-Bel UK Ltd; Derek Bloom, Sean Carroll and Katie Turner – (Batchelors) Brooke Bond Foods Ltd; Kirsty MacEachen – (Bovril & Marmite) CPC (UK) Ltd; Michael Thornton – Thorntons plc; Stephen Ward – Cadbury Schweppes plc; James Robertson – Robertson's Orkney Ltd; Patricia Melville – (Stockans) Tod Holdings Ltd; John Mutch – Princes Foods Ltd; Kevin Lawton – Quaker Oats Ltd; Peter MacDonald – The Body Shop; Survival Suits – W. M. Supplies (UK) Ltd.

9

With thanks for help and advice on their kit: Frank Goodman and Robin Goodliffe – Valley Canoe Products; David Patrick – P & H Company; Andy Bowman – Wild Country Ltd.

Robin Denniston of Denniston & Lownie literary agents for persuading me to write this book; and finally to Maggie Body at Hodder & Stoughton, for encouragement, editing and hours of work to make this book happen.

Contents

Prologue
July 1990

"My god, he's over," I shouted. Now just keep calm and concentrate, or you'll be over too, I told myself, feeling unsteady and tense.

I tried to relax and keep my slender craft pointing into the swell. The uninviting, cold salt water off Handa Island see-sawed around me. I must keep close to the other two canoes. If I capsized now there would be no one to rescue me from my potential watery death trap.

Nigel had already pulled Dad's canoe across his own and begun to tip the water out, while Dad hung spluttering on to the front of Nigel's canoe, losing his delicate sense of balance as the cold water sapped his energy. All the time they were being pulled closer to the foaming reef.

I could see Dad's paddle floating away on the lead-coloured sea. Maybe I could pick it up and take it back to him? If I tried to shout to Nigel he might not hear or, worse, think I was in trouble, too. Surely I could use what little skill I had to do something to help. I carefully turned my canoe broadside to the swell and nosed slowly forward, eyes fixed on the paddle in the water ahead. Reaching it, I hastily grabbed the shaft and, with shaking hands, turned it so that the blades lay at the same angle as my own. It wasn't going to be easy to paddle.

Then I was over. The cold bubbling salt water engulfed me, I kept my lips firmly closed and held my breath as I struggled to free the spraydeck, bumping and bruising my legs whilst trying to escape to the light above. With my head above the surface, I made sure I grabbed the two paddles in one arm and held tightly on to my upturned canoe with the other hand. I no longer felt frightened, I was excited. I was part of the sea, it held me, and could do with me what it chose.

I searched the surface of the water for Nigel's red canoe; it was nowhere to be seen. I was sure he would come back for me, all I had to do was stay clear of the reef. I hoped Dad was all right. The waves that broke over the under-water reef looked much larger from this level, and I was definitely getting closer. I tried to swim backwards, towing my canoe and paddles, searching the surface of the water for Nigel.

"You all right?" his unflustered voice enquired.

"I'm fine."

"Well, just hold on to the cord at the end of my canoe and we'll have you back in here in a tick."

"Is Dad okay?"

"Yes, he should be at the shore by now."

Nigel pulled my canoe over his front deck and tipped the water out, while I disentangled myself from a panic brush with a lobster creel line. I was getting cold, I had been in the water quite long enough. As soon as my canoe was empty, Nigel put it in the water next to his and held tightly on to it.

"You'll have to get in quickly, and I'll steer us away from the reef," he said over his shoulder. I held on to the back of both canoes, pushing down with my arms and lifting my legs out of the water, before slithering like a beetle stuck on its back towards my own cockpit, keeping the body weight low to hold the craft stable. Then Nigel steered us past the foaming reef into a wide rocky bay. Once behind a natural breakwater the surface of the sea was flat. I spotted Dad and waved to him. He sat on a seaweed-covered rock, looking glumly down at his beached craft.

On the footpath above the shore, stood several bird-watchers. Dressed in neutral colours, with day-sack or a canvas bag slung over one shoulder containing reference books and lunch, they stopped briefly, leaning on well-cared-for walking sticks to peer through good quality binoculars at the drowned rats washed up on the shore. The fact that we were close to hypothermia and had survived a potentially fatal incident probably made them even more scathing about our treacherous sport. Like fishermen, bird-watchers must feel that canoeists cause a disturbance.

I paddled the last bit to the shore and gingerly stepped out, teeth chattering, soaked, and minus one of my cross-country running shoes which I had kicked off while paddling.

"Oh Nigel, what do we do now?" Dad asked jokingly, through frozen lips, trying to put a brave face on what was beginning to look like a tricky situation. We still had to paddle the five miles back to Ardmore. It was decided that while we changed into dry things and walked across to the sheltered side of the island, Nigel would tow our canoes round the headland. We watched the expert set off alone into waves that made his canoe bounce like a cork. Our lesson in sea kayaking temporarily suspended, Dad and I walked over the island. A great skua circled above, waiting to outwit some feebler prey. I hoped it had not noticed our weakened state.

At the sandy bay there was Nigel, holding up my missing shoe, which he had managed to save in the surf. What a star he was proving to be. We got back into our damp canoes, with sand stuck to our wet feet, and paddled along the calmer south side of Handa Island. How different its gently shelving pale sandy beaches leading into turquoise shallows were after the hostile west with its dark 200 foot sandstone cliffs hemmed by surf from the ever aggressive North Atlantic. Paddling north through the Sound of Handa we were sheltered, but the wind was getting up all the time from the south-west, and the swell would be rising. To the west I could see the vast expanse of sea stretching to the invisible Isle of Lewis, no place to be with the weather worsening and little skill or experience. We must get back to the sheltered waters of Loch Laxford and into Loch a'Chadh-Fi, which is always protected from the cruel sea swell.

We paddled through the shelter of the small islands just north of Tarbet, a group of croft houses, none of which have been spared the loss of one or more of their menfolk in the sea around Handa. Thrust out into the jubbly water, I began to feel as unsteady as I had done just before the capsize. I knew Dad must be feeling wobbly too. It would not be good to go in again. We turned to follow the coastline north. Spray beat against the pink and white Lewisian gneiss, contorted from heat and pressure millions of years before, leaping high to threaten precarious clumps of heather. Was there a parallel between these wiry plants and us? Dark clouds loomed all around, what had begun as a still sunny summer's day was quickly becoming more menacing. I concentrated fiercely, not wanting to be the first to go in, and desperate to show the other two that I could do it, that I had the stamina to keep going and, with practice, I would improve.

"Rebecca, can you raft up with John." Though Nigel spoke quietly, this was not so much a question as a direction. I was more used to orders being barked at me. I paddled carefully closer to Dad, knowing that he could easily pull me in. We bumped together clumsily and held on tight, now we were a stable raft. "I think it's best if I tow you now," said Nigel, clipping his tow-line on to the cord loops at the front of our canoes. We were like a dead battleship being towed into its final resting place!

Nigel paddled two lengths ahead of us. With the following sea, each swell took us surfing towards him, narrowly missing our rescuer. Just before we reached the mouth of Loch Laxford, Nigel turned his head and said, "Are you sure you want to canoe round Cape Horn *this* winter?"

Cape Horn and its notorious sailing graveyard tend to come up in our family. My father had first hoped to sail round it in his 30-foot sloop *English Rose IV* in the course of the Golden Globe single-handed non-stop round the world race in 1968–9. But a collision before the start led to him having to retire to the Brazilian coast. Nine years later, in the 1977–8 Whitbread Round the World Race, he and my mother rounded the Horn together aboard their 57-foot ketch *English Rose VI* (renamed *Debenhams* for the race). They were part of a crew of twelve heading for Rio and the final leg back to Portsmouth. Then, in January 1985, Dad did it again in the same boat with just Andy Briggs. This time the pair of them were making a record 203-day non-stop circumnavigation. Sailing half a mile out in 70 knot gusts, Cape Horn's 1400-foot cliffs were their first sight of land since the Canaries shortly after they had set out.

Conspicuous challenges, there to be grasped and measured up against, are part of growing up with my father. He is always urging us to seize the moment and live life to the full. Now it was my turn. I was twenty-three and I wanted to achieve something amazing. Being the first woman to paddle a kayak round Cape Horn Island fitted the bill. This is what the sea-kayaking training with Nigel Dennis was in aid of. Canoeing had become serious.

Not that life had lacked its excitements hitherto. Looking back over it, as far as I can remember there has always been something brewing or going on, usually with my father barking exhortations or encouragement in the middle of it. In writing the story from my own perspective, I have tried to avoid dwelling too much on the territory both my parents have already covered in their own books, stories about the early days of their Adventure School and the adoption of my sister Elizabeth, though of course I do not want to avoid these altogether, nor can I. But there was plenty of new ground to cover in Peru where our travels in the narco country of the Amazon headwaters, dodging Shining Path terrorists in 1989, gave me a sobering insight into a world where life is held cheap, but also a taste of adrenalin-pumping adventure.

Part One
ARDMORE

I

Daughter of the Croft

I was brought to Ardmore in a fish basket at the age of three weeks, aboard an open rowing boat. I had been born nine months after my father landed his twenty-foot dory, *English Rose III* on the Aran Islands. He and Chay Blyth had just rowed the Atlantic. A baby race ensued and I narrowly beat Samantha Blyth, arriving on 3 July 1967, looking out like a particularly shrivelled prune from the now faded front page of the *Daily Mail*.

I was a happy baby, taken everywhere with my parents, and had the obliging habit of sleeping solidly during car journeys, or at other people's houses. My ex-SAS father was rather wary of me, in case I might break. He saw himself more as a provider than a nappy-changer and had brought his young city-bred wife and child to begin their own SAS training course in the harshest place he could find on the mainland of Britain.

Ardmore consisted of a scatter of crofts, half of them abandoned, on the steep side of a sea loch fifteen miles south of Cape Wrath in the north-west corner of Scotland. I did not think it remarkable to be brought up in such a remote place. In fact, I did not think of it as remote. It was my world, the place I loved most and where I was most loved. We had no electricity, so no television; no road, so no car outside the door. It took a long time to get anywhere and we did so by boat across Loch a'Chadh-Fi, a northerly arm of Loch Laxford, with careful reference to the tide if loading or unloading.

Just as I took this stormswept idyll as the norm, my father's recent fame was also a fact of life. As a child I had often looked at the heavy metal printer's plate of the front page of the *People* which the newspaper had given Dad as a souvenir. "Frank, Fearless and Free", read the *People*'s motto. Sunday, 4 September 1966. The headline read, "Atlantic rowers land in Galway Bay. THEY'VE MADE IT!" Sub-headings pro-claimed, "Tired, they said 'No' to a tot", "Dazed", and "Delighted". There was a photograph of Dad and Mum with Chay and his wife Maureen, and another of the pair rowing, as well as a map of Ireland to show where they had landed. Of course I was proud that this was about my father, but I was more interested in trying to decipher the other front-page stories: "Susie's mini-skirt shocks a town's coppers" and "Mrs Roberts' strip pulls in the crowds" next to an advertisement for Marmite.

Beside the front page of the *People* always stood a fine silver model of an oar, mounted on a piece of greeny-grey Connemara marble which had been given to Dad by a lady who had lost her dearly loved brother at sea. For my parents these items must have been reminders of des-perate worry and moments of great joy. They were always there during my childhood. I did not know why they were kept side by side. But I used to like to trace my index finger along the silver oar, and feel the smooth marble base. I had yet to discover its deeper significance.

I grew up at Number 76 Ardmore and moved back in to it two years ago. (The curiously suburban-sounding house-numbering records the order in which they were built and noted down in the vast Sutherland parish of Eddrachilles.) My memories of Number 76 are strong and true. I imagined it would be my home for ever. I used to play with the son of my parents' early partners in the Adventure School they set up. Jamie Liddon was the same age as me, but a lot tougher. He never wore shoes, scampering across the rocks on his bruised cut feet, and he would pick up pieces of glass with no fear that they might cut him. He liked to play with his few toys in a burn close to the wooden house at the bottom of the hill. I sometimes took some of my toys down to play with him, as we got on well until the incident of the stuffed sheep. This was my favourite toy, which most people thought was a rabbit. It wore a blue-and-white checked dress, and there was a baby lamb tucked under its left arm. Jamie either did not like the lamb or thought it was dead, as he buried it. After this Mum tried to keep me busy close by her side.

The first season at the Adventure School began on 5 July 1969. I was two years old, almost to the day, and still having to be transported in a rucksack for long walking journeys, but well away in my red wellies for anything shorter. When Dad was not too busy, he would lift me high on to his shoulders and carry me through the wood which separated Upper and Lower Ardmore, letting me steer him by pulling his ears. But with Dad busy running the courses and Mum feeding up to fifty people at a time on a single peat-fired Rayburn, I was often left to my own devices and found a wonderful place to play. The walls of Number 76 were three feet thick. I could stand up easily on the deep windowsill and by pulling the curtains together I had a secret place to arrange my teddy bears and conduct imaginary tea parties. The croft house seemed plenty big enough to me, but tall men who entered were forever bumping their heads. Most of my childhood seems to have been in an imaginary world. I talked to myself a lot of the time when I was playing on my own. The Liddons left after two seasons and then I was the only child at Ardmore. I did not miss other children, as I had never really known play with others of my own age.

The small white wooden porch of Number 76 was close to collapse, but its rotten sills housed many geraniums, the scent from their bruised leaves always filling the air. My mother's love for gardening and growing plants is something she has passed on to me. Outside, under the step, lived a large toad, who appeared from his damp home to search for grubs and feel the warmth of the sun on his warty skin. There was also a brass handbell for visitors to sound their arrival and me to ring if I needed someone to open the door for me.

Spring comes late to the north-west corner of Scotland and sometimes Mum and I might celebrate it by rowing out to a'Chadh-Fi island with a picnic. Mum would lie amongst the primroses enjoying the spring sun, while I scratted around on the shore, waking her to show her what I had found, or standing in her sun! Before it got too late, we would return with great bunches of primroses and I would spend hours making posies and filling bowls with moss and the pale yellow flowers to decorate the supper tables for the people on the courses, who would return weary and hungry from their day on the hill, or canoeing or sailing.

As I grew, I was allowed to roam free, along the shoreline, into the wood to pick bluebells, over the croft and up on to the rugged hill behind the house, returning when I got hungry or wet! It was a perfect early childhood, with plenty of love, food, fresh air and exercise.

Next door, at Number 77, lived the Ross family. There had been Rosses at Ardmore for longer than anyone could remember. Granny Ross had been brought to the house as a young bride – from Number

76 next door. Now her bachelor sons, Hughie and Heckie, tended the sheep and her daughters, Bessy and Molly, took turns at keeping house for them and working on the east coast. I used to love to help Heckie Ross at haymaking. He and his devoted collie, Mona, would keep the sheep off their inbye land after lambing, letting the grass grow long and to seed. Then Heckie would scythe it in slow wide sweeps, Mona sitting close by, watching her master's every move. The freshly cut grass would then have to be raked, and I would scamper backwards and forwards with sweet-smelling armfuls, throwing them on to the stack, as Heckie continued at his own peaceful rate. After a few days, the grass, now turning to hay, would be forked over, so the bottom of the pile had a chance to dry, and several turnings later, Heckie would carry great bundles up to the byre to feed the sheep in winter.

To Heckie, there never seemed to be any panic. He always moved slowly, and could often be spotted leaning on his stick, smoking another cigarette. His mother or sister would give a sharp blast on the whistle, a sign that dinner was ready, and Heckie would slowly make his way back to the croft. He was religious, as were all the family, and spent many long winter evenings reading the Bible by the light of the Tilley lamp.

During lambing, there would usually be a few orphans who had to be hand-fed and became great pets. Molly or Bessy would bottle-feed, while Heckie and Hughie patrolled the hills twice a day to look for new births. We often wondered how these wretched little creatures would survive when born on the top of a hill in an early spring snowstorm. There was a scarecrow up there to keep the birds away, but new lambs were often taken by crows, buzzards and foxes. I loved to feel the young lambs sucking on my thumb and the tight woollen curls of their coats. One such pet was named Millie, after being hand-reared on Millac (the powdered milk we drink). She remained a pet, and would walk over to welcome people and let me ride on her back. I wanted to be a shepherdess, like in the story books. I was soon to discover this was a less pretty profession than the nursery rhymes let on. But it never put me off, and now I am one.

Hughie Ross moved away to Inverness, married a nurse and became a painter and decorator. There was not enough work for him at Ardmore. In 1979, Heckie had a massive coronary, followed by several more minor attacks, and died. I was away at boarding school by then, but remember being deeply shocked and crying when Mum told me the news over the telephone. Quiet, gentle Heckie was so much a part of Ardmore; his steadiness belonged to the old Ardmore that could not return. Granny Ross was heartbroken and died the same year. With Heckie and Granny Ross both gone, there was no reason for any of the Ross family to stay at Ardmore. Heckie's sheep were sold at the Lairg sales. I had never known the place without sheep, no fresh wool on the broken fences and nothing to keep down the grass.

My parents made a plan to improve the inbye land around the croft, to refence, cut the bracken and scrub back to the croft boundaries, replenish the over-grazed ground with lime and to buy a small number of fresh stock. As the crofting way of life was dying out, there were grants available for anyone who wished to keep their land in good condition or to improve it. So sheep returned to Ardmore.

Each autumn we would slaughter a couple of cast ewes, female sheep that are too old to lamb and have started to lose their teeth. These would provide enough mutton for the winter months when it was often impossible to cross the loch for supplies. Bobby Mcleod, Molly's husband, came out to show us how it was done. He had been a shepherd all his life. As directed by Bobby, we put the ewe into the old schoolhouse, a corrugated-iron one-roomed building down by the shore beyond the Rosses' croft. It had been used to store lobster creels and for butchering ever since its school lessons ended, when there were no young left at Ardmore.

The ewe was starved for twenty-four hours to empty its stomach. Bobby showed us the tools we would need for the task: a small sharp rigid knife, a saw, an empty salmon-food bag, a pail and a saucepan. Nothing must be wasted. With great deftness, Bobby got on with the business of killing the beast. With its front legs tied to one hind leg, it was lifted on to the table, belly uppermost and head hanging over one end. Bobby's small knife was then taken to the jugular. I held the beast down and looked away, focusing my eyes on Ben Stack, which I could see through a crack in the rusting wall. The ewe struggled for a second. I pushed hard down on its breast bone and haunch, then the hollow trickling sound of its blood landing in the chipped enamel pail below and the limpness of the beast relieved me; it could feel no pain. When the jugular is cut, the heart continues to pump the blood for nearly five minutes, thus making the gutting of the beast much cleaner. The pail of blood is quickly removed before the last trickle, so that no vomit mixes with it, which would ruin the black pudding; a dessertspoon of salt is then added to help it congeal.

Bobby talked us through every step, Dad taking meticulous notes, which he would later type up and fablonise for our own butchering sessions. I was obviously going to be the butcher's mate. No one else was keen to do it. I did not mind so much once the head was cut off. Then it did not seem quite like an animal. But the brown watery eyes and flared nostrils of terror were hard to ignore, and kept me concentrating fiercely on the glimpse of Ben Stack through the crack in the wall.

Once the beast is dead, it must be dealt with quickly before becoming cold and harder to work. The main worry is puncturing the stomach, which is easy to do when cutting the skin down the centre of the belly or sawing through the breast bone. Sawing, skinning, pulling, peeling, by turn vigorously and cautiously, you get to the suet (for black or white pudding), on the way to the heart, kidneys, liver and chops.

In the old days everyone used their own meat, not the delicious-looking but tasteless red meat, pumped full of hormones and water, you can buy in the supermarket. It did raise a few eyebrows though, when back at school on Monday I would write in my newsbook what I had been doing at the weekend!

2

Lance and Ada

When I was three, Lance and Ada Bell came to live at Ardmore from Teesside where Lance was a foreman over forty-five men in the general-engineering department of a Stockton iron foundry. Now their children were grown up they could please themselves and an article about the Adventure School in the *Daily Telegraph* prompted Lance to write and offer his services. Lance was a perfectionist who could turn his hand to making or mending almost anything, and Ardmore suited his pioneering independent spirit.

During the war Ada had been a crane driver in the foundry where Lance worked. He had spotted her from ground level because she was "the best operator I'd ever seen", he fondly remembers. This is by far from being the only talent Ada possesses. If I could bake, knit and sew the things Ada does to half her standard, I would not be doing badly. Ada always had time to show me what she was doing, and make me feel useful. I would be invited to stamp on sheets in the bath and then help rush them out to the old mangle in the byre, where I could hold the dripping end up out of the peat dross, as I was not yet big enough to turn the handle.

The Bells' arrival was perfect timing for me and I was always walking up through the wood from Lower Ardmore to Upper Ardmore to see Ada at Number 80, or the Blue House as it became once Hughie Ross painted it. For a long while I could not do this on my own, as I was rather afraid. Ada had to "set me back" until I could see our house and then I would run on alone, waving to her when I reached the gate safely. Or Mum would walk part of the way up with me. The thing I was worried about was the small stone house on the edge of our croft. The narrow path runs right in front of it. This was where Ninnie lived. She was more than a little strange, a small woman with a tangle of grey hair, her face covered in flour, dressed in old tattered skirts, a piece of string around her waist holding her jangling keys, baggy lisle stockings falling in wrinkles around her ankles and sturdy boots. She spent most of her day stomping backwards and forwards through the wood to the old public phone box, which no longer worked as the phone had been moved into Number 76. Once there, she would make a few imaginary calls and return home, stopping periodically to begin a mad dance round and round, while she laughed and sang to herself. When you passed her house, missiles such as tea leaves or water were often hurled out of the door. I could not help but think of her as a witch. Poor old Ninnie seemed to fit every story-book description of witches, except for the black cat. After safely passing Ninnie's, I would enter the wood with heart pounding, imagination running riot, which is ironic considering Ardmore must have been one of the safest places, and still is, for a child to grow up. There is no fear of abduction or rape or a traffic accident there on a dark night.

Sometimes I would stay the night with Lance and Ada. I always looked forward to this; Ada made a delicious supper of Yorkshire puddings, cooked in a set of blackened round tins that fitted one inside the other, and eaten traditionally as a separate course – mine had syrup on it, while they preferred gravy. This would be followed by meat and sweet home-grown vegetables, then a delicious sensible pudding. Rice pudding was a favourite with nutmeg and a blob of home-made black-currant jam. After the washing-up, Ada and I would curl up in a large wicker chair under a woollen rug in front of the pot-bellied stove, and she would read to me. *Little House on the Prairie* and *The Borrowers* were two of our favourites. Every now and then, Lance would give the Tilley lamp a few more pumps, occasionally interrupting to ask a question about the story which I would answer, feeling pleased with myself that I had been paying more attention than he! He would not be sitting idle whilst listening, but sorting out seeds for planting, writing letters or mending something for the house.

When my eyelids began to droop, Ada would suggest bed and I would insist on one more page, before she took me upstairs to the landing where, under the skylight in the eaves, I would climb into my shaky down, made from the sofa cushions, blankets and sheets, always smooth and ironed. If it was winter, I would have a hot-water bottle, and a small paraffin lamp left close by so that it was not too dark. In the summer, the light still shone through the skylight. Often the sheep "baa'd" at each other all night, as Heckie used the field in front of the Blue House to separate the lambs from the ewes before they went to the sale.

Lance has old-fashioned, well-tested remedies for everything. He puts sheep's wool between his toes to protect his corns, takes regular swigs of cod-liver oil from the bottle when winter is coming, and on extra-cold mornings has a tot of fiery liquid from the cupboard in the other room which holds rows of screw-top bottles containing Ada's home-brewed beer. He eats plenty of dripping on his bread, loves pickled onions and beetroot, and still has total contempt for any foreign or "mucked on with" food.

Lance made me a pair of wooden stilts, which I practised on for weeks until I got the hang of them, and on one of my birthdays, he put up a swing by the washing line. There was a large rock behind the swing which you could climb to get a good push off, then you had to be careful not to bump your feet on it each time you swung backwards. The rope was the same blue nylon rope, used for the running moorings, that the cows at the end of the loch loved to chew. When frayed it became brittle and splintered into my soft palms, so Ada taped on pieces of foam to allow me to hold on in comfort. I loved that swing.

In the early summer I would help with the peat cutting. At first I could only straighten the peats once Ada had lifted them on to the bank, but when I grew a bit, I could lift them out of the trench myself. I loved getting dirty and squelching around in the gluey brown mush in the bottom of the trench. I think Lance liked the muck too. We would return black, to show how hard we had been working. A few weeks later the peats needed turning, then stacking, before we could carry them back to the byre when they were really dry. I had my own small sack, and each time we got down from the top of the hill past the water tank to the byre, we chalked up another mark on the back of the byre door, four in a row and one across.

If Ada was not out carrying the peats too, she would be busy inside. I do not think I have ever arrived at the front door to see Ada sitting doing nothing. Any old clothes could be turned into something useful, material kept for patches, buttons, poppers and zips kept to replace others. Cotton or other natural-fibre clothes were given to Lance to wrap his tools in, old leather boots were used to make washers. Outgrown hand-knitted jumpers would be unravelled, rewound and knitted into something else. It was Ada who taught me to knit, when I wanted to make a long scarf for Dad and I always used to love to play with the multi-coloured contents of her knitting-needle box, made by Lance's father.

Lance's father had been a keen vegetable gardener, and so was Lance, who showed me how to plant potatoes, radishes, lettuces, cabbages, carrots, turnips, beetroot, spring onions, peas and beans, the latter two coated in poisonous red lead, to deter the mice. Lance could eat a couple of heads of lettuce at a sitting, but he often felt drowsy after this, like the Flopsy Bunnies in Mr McGregor's rubbish heap. Later we found out that lettuce is full of laudanum; or as Beatrix Potter observed, "eating too much lettuce is 'soporific'."

Later in the year we would drink Ada's home-made elderflower champagne out in the garden between picking pounds and pounds of blackcurrants, which had to be quickly made into pies and jam before they went bad. There were no freezers at Ardmore for many years until the electricity came.

Ada's hens supplied plenty of free-range eggs. The cockerel terrorised Upper Ardmore, guarding his ladies and territory, which happened to be a stretch of the path. I knew to run whenever he came after me, but others who tried to stand up to him often got off the worse.

What I always wanted to have was a pet seagull, and for a couple of years I tried to rear one from a chick. They lived in a box in the porch but the poor little balls of grey fluff never survived very long. Maybe we did not feed them on the right things. I wanted my chick to grow into a handsome, brilliant-white gull which would stand on the gate post and fly above me as I walked around, or settle on the prow of my boat. Alas, it was not to be.

We used to go in the *Ada Bell*, Lance's boat, down to the seagull island to collect eggs for cooking. We went early in the season, so that the gulls had time to lay another clutch. So well camouflaged were the eggs and nests that we must have missed plenty. It was like an Easter egg hunt, but for real. Eider also nested on the island but we never took their pale greeny-grey eggs. Back on the boat, we would test the gulls' eggs in a bucket of water. If they floated, they were no good and throwing the floaters at the rocks to smash them was the best fun of the whole trip. Egg-collecting has been done for centuries by the Highlanders who live along the coast, and their occasional bucketfuls are never enough to upset the delicate balance of nature.

If the hens were Ada's, Lance took to sheep. He rescued some very weak lambs from Portlevorchy at the head of the loch, which became known as the "white mice of Ardmore", but not for long; Lance had a vision of large healthy sheep fit to win first prize in a show. He tended to their every need, and built them up with breakfast, lunch and supper. They spent cold nights in the byre. Potato peelings were specially dried in the Rayburn and fed to the lambs with flaked maize and plenty of hay. One or two of the small lambs were beyond recovery, but the rest grew into titanic sheep, with whom Lance then had to wrestle to shear and dip.

When I was five the Sutherland Education Authority sent their primary adviser out to Ardmore to discuss how I could be educated. It was clear that there was no chance of me going up the coast to Kinlochbervie each day, a three-mile walk and a twenty-minute bus journey at the beginning and end of each day. I was too young to lodge with a family away from home. It was a bit of a problem, until the primary adviser saw how well Ada and I got on. He suggested that she do a crash course on the east coast to become a primary teacher. Ada was amazed at this, having never thought of becoming a teacher, but she had a natural ability to teach in a way that did not seem like one was being taught. So in the summer of 1972, Mrs Bell's Academy for Young Ladies opened in the Blue House. I was the first and only pupil.

I had a satchel, and trotted off up through the wood to school with Ada every weekday. Lessons were held in the sitting-room. Exercise books, pencils and a huge box of "Chub" coloured crayons were supplied by the school at Kinlochbervie. We had a small blackboard and the walls were covered with paintings and drawings. Ada taught me to read, write and do sums but she also taught me to make bread, bottle beer, look for birds' nests, sink tins in the loch, and never waste anything.

Whilst Ada taught me at the Bell Academy for Young Ladies at Ardmore, we visited the local primary school at Kinlochbervie once every few weeks. This was to help me get used to other children, and what a normal school was like. The plan was for me to go when I was seven, to be a weekly boarder, lodging with Mrs Rookes, the lady teacher.

Although close as the crow flies, Kinlochbervie was a lifetime away. Kinlochbervie had electricity, which I had hardly come across before, television, street lights, roads and cars, even a travelling shop. All this was new to me.

I began my week by walking out along the mile and a half of winding hilly path to the school bus which came to pick me up on Monday morning. My stomach felt heavy as we travelled towards school, picking up children of various age, height, size and cleanliness along the route. There was always a lot of noise in the bus. My English accent slipped gently into a Scottish one without my even knowing it.

The old girls mothered me, as I was shy and frightened of everything going on around. I had missed out on the first two years of bond-making, and now had to get myself into an already established group. In our class of six, "the wee ones", the other two girls, Fiona and Angela, were both intelligent and extremely hard working, already determined to achieve careers and make their way in a wider world. Two of the boys were less enthusiastic, though the third, Dominic, son of Mr Burgess the English peripatetic music master, was bright and keen. So in class it usually became a case of the three bright ones battling for supremacy, and the three not so bright, myself included, struggling to keep up.

Mrs Rookes, with whom I stayed, looked as if she worked too hard and needed a good break. Her often tired face counted for the hours of preparation and marking she had put in to make sure her children got the best education she could possibly give them. She smelt of cigarette smoke and often sounded a bit chesty, either from too many cigarettes or all the bugs brought into school by us brats she tried to break in to learning. She was calm, steady and patient, but had definite standards to which we had to measure up. I respected her greatly. We chanted our tables and went up to Mrs Rookes' desk to do our reading, and every Friday had a spelling test. Each day we wrote in our newsbook and drew a picture underneath with wax crayons.

Mr Marshall the headmaster terrified us wee ones, as he had had a stroke, and one side of his face had fallen, giving him a rather frightening look and a large red eye. It was difficult to understand what he said at first, but he was always joking, unless forced into a rage by someone kicking a football through one of his windows. Then, out came the belt, and he would line up the guilty ones for punishment in front of the class. Pieces of chalk and blackboard rubbers were also liable to be hurled by Mr Marshall at any of the older children caught not concentrating in his class.

As well as the three "R's" we were taught art, sewing and music. We all looked forward to singing lessons from Mr Burgess. At Christmas he gave us sweet-smelling photocopied paper with carols in purple writing on them. We played the recorder with Mr Burgess too, but the noise was so terrible, I was discouraged from playing mine at home. Maybe this is why I never became very good. Sometimes a kilted old gentleman appeared to teach some of the older children to play the chanter, which is the beginning of learning to play the bagpipes. His chanter pupils were the most musical children in the school, so they held their noses in the air when with him.

Sewing was not too highly thought of by most of the boys, but they still had to do it. We started by sewing dot-to-dot on cards, then progressed to basic tapestry. I remember the cones of wool lined up, and the decisiveness with which we knew what colours we wanted to use. There was little doubt about choice in those early years.

When Mrs Rookes' daughter went to secondary school on the east coast, and I spent more and more time playing with the Burgess children, it was decided that I should stay with them instead. They lived next door to Mrs Rookes in the other school house. I became "Reb", instead of "Becca" because they had a Rebecca already. Then there was "Domo" who was in my class, and "Milla" two classes above us. Becca and I shared a room downstairs. She was small and prone to sulking, probably driven to it by her brother and sister. Domo and I got on well, but Milla liked to rule the roost, and often gave us a hard time! I was frightened of her for a long while. We walked the dog, laid the table, washed, dried up and cleared away every day, in a rota system, the plan for which hung in the kitchen close to the Potterton boiler, where their cat "Potterton" always slept. We had penny wafers for break, ate lots of sandwich spread, white fish with fennel seeds (which I did not like), and Camilla had to eat Nimble bread as she was rather plump. We were allowed to watch the television news, *Tomorrow's World* and *It's a Knock Out* only. Advanced viewing for a seven-year-old.

School reports were boringly average and steady. I had no particular talent, but I was not too stupid either. The number of pupils increased, and another teacher was taken on. Miss Mackay had been a missionary in Africa. Her mother ran the local shop and her brother ran the travelling shop, so between them, they had the market sewn up. Miss Mackay was very religious and strict, she expected us to work hard, and the thing I will always remember Miss Mackay for is holding a small girl up in the air by her feet and smacking her bottom in front of the class. I do not know what little Rhona had done, but she certainly would not do it again. In fact, all our behaviour improved after this example.

3

Fish Lessons

In summer and autumn from dusk onwards you can often hear the haunting bark of seals in Loch Laxford, almost like wolves conversing through the night air. The pups are a pale gingery brown, and sometimes do not survive a severe winter storm, becoming separated from their mothers. I once found an injured pup north of Ardmore at Sandwood Bay; the strong on-shore wind had brought it in on the huge surf and it lay partially covered by wind-blown sand. I had no fish to give it, and thought it might stand a better chance of survival if moved into a more sheltered spot. But the pup growled and tried to bite when I came too close, so I covered it with more sand instead of moving it. I doubt it survived.

Canoeing out at Ardmore Point, through the turbulent narrow gap between two small rocky islets, I have often seen seals playing in the surf and fishing. The sea bed is sandy here, with large leafy kelp growing upwards like trees. I have seen the dark form of seals swimming under my boat. Luckily they are still a little too wary to give me a playful nudge and tip me in.

Sadly, when you become a salmon farmer, as we did, you have to see seals in a different light. The earliest salmon farms were constructed with one single net, hung from a square cage. The seals simply swam up under the net, causing the fish to panic and dive to the waiting seal who could suck out the fish's liver through the net, leaving the remains to rot. Sometimes nets were torn and all the fish swam away. Then the salmon farmers discovered that if a second larger net was placed around the outside of the net which held the fish, with a few-feet gap between the two, and weighted so that it hung vertically in the water, this would make it impossible for the lone seal to get at the fish. But the seals outsmarted us again by starting to work in pairs. One would swim under

33

the lower net, and push it up until the outer and inner nets touched. The fish then dived as usual, and the second seal could get to them. They also learnt to attack at night when all we could do was watch from the shore, catching a glimpse of a sleek head in the moonlight. You could hear them breathing.

To begin with, we did not know whether it was seals or shags killing the fish. Every day globules of oil floated to the surface, and on lifting the net, we found tens and hundreds of dead fish rotting at the bottom. In desperation we began to lift the nets each day, to see what destruction had been done the night before. They were fresh fish now, so we bought four chest freezers and ran them off a generator. Anything was better than letting these fish go to waste. Once the freezers were full Mum started smoking the fish.

Dad taught us both to shoot the .303 rifle, which was kept locked away in Mum's dress cupboard. We could not carry on like this. I remember lying in my bed and hearing my parents discussing the future downstairs in the kitchen. "If this goes on much longer, we just won't be able to afford to keep Bec at school." I lay motionless, holding my breath to hear what was to happen next. Although I had always longed for the holidays, it was a shock to hear them talk like this. At the age of ten or eleven, somehow you feel that however bad it gets, your parents will work it out in the end, grown-ups always do. Luckily, Dad came up with the idea of lowering the outer net until its bottom was ten feet below the bottom of the inner net with the salmon in. The seals couldn't lift the outer net and all the weights, so they gave up. We had won, but it meant I realised from an early age how everything was a struggle, especially in our precarious outpost. It was like being a settler in the Wild West.

I spent most of my school holidays from the age of nine or ten helping on the salmon farm. It was too small to justify a fulltime employee, so we all mucked in to help. In the summer, I walked down from our croft house to the shore through buttercups and clover, then wading chest-high through bracken, its strong waxy stems parting like a green sea. At the running mooring I would pull in the boat and haul myself towards the raft of cages, checking for red stinging jellyfish tentacles on the rope, whilst listening to the splashing silver fish. The fish food was kept in a garden shed on the raft. Three black buckets would empty one sack, first filling the feeders which hung from scaffolding poles over the middle of the cages, and then feeding each cage of fish by hand, until they stopped rising to the surface. It was crucial not to feed too quickly, as some of the pellets would surely fall through the bottom and sides of the net to the waiting wild cuddies. I stood up on the middle bar of the cage side, resting my knees on the top bar to support myself. This enabled me to throw pellets well into the centre of the cage. As the first handful hit the water, hungry fish turned and headed vertically for the surface which soon boiled with silver salmon desperate to get their share. There were usually one or two blind fish in each cage whose eyes had been damaged by hitting the net. They swam round and round the edge of the net, bumping into corners. I would throw a few pellets in front of them, so they could hardly miss if they kept their mouths open. They were black and became thin and covered with sea lice, usually ending up as supper for our spoilt cats. The smell and dust from the fish food permeated all outer clothing, and stuck in ever short fingernails.

When I had school friends staying we spent hours out on the cages fishing for cuddies with mussel-flesh bait. One summer, a great shoal of larger cuddies swam into the loch, and suddenly we could reach out and touch fish ten times the size of the small ones we had been catching. This caused pandemonium, as my fishing companion and I screamed with delight, abandoned our short lines and went at them direct with the landing net. As I whirled the long heavy handle round in the air I narrowly missed sending my best friend to join the miraculous draught.

Granny Ross was still alive, but could not move from her chair. She loved visits from us young children, and we would take her the small cuddies, fresh from the sea. "Get the sweetie tin down," she would say to Molly or Bessy. The choice was invariably liquorice-and-blackcurrant wrapped sweets, orange or mint pan-drops. I preferred the former, but they all tasted slightly of mint. Granny Ross would listen to our tales of excitement during the fishing trip, of how we had accidentally filled our wellies with seawater, or lost our hooks, and how many we had each caught. She always said she loved the sweet taste of the small fish better than the larger ones, though maybe she said this to encourage us.

One of my jobs on the fish farm was to count the salmon when they were sorted and graded. This involved sitting under the blue wooden sorting board with pencil and paper marking down under different columns what I heard my father shout out. It was often a long cold job, trying to protect my paper from drips of rain and fish slime, but it

35

was an important one, and had to be accurate. We would sort the salmon from the grilse. These are fish that mature after one year in seawater, becoming larger, more chunky in shape, and brownish rather than bright silver. As the price for them is not so good, we always hoped there would not be too many. I knew there would be a lot of glum days to follow, if my columns totted up to anything more than one quarter grilse.

Collecting fish food from Laxford pier at high tide was always good fun. I steered the fishing boat, *Ardmore Rose*, standing on a box so that I could see out of the wheelhouse windows, past Weaver's Bay with its old iron mooring rings used by ships departing for America with the dispossessed of the Highland Clearances. Laxford pier is close to the road, and can be driven on to by a lorry. It belongs to the Duke of Westminster, and is strongly constructed from huge blocks of rock, held together by a thick metal band.

While the strong young instructors who worked at the Adventure School for a summer season unloaded the 25-kilo bags, I played on the beach. It was close to the mouth of the Laxford river, and quite different from the beaches at Ardmore, with small grey flat stones which were good for skimming. There was also a hollow drain which ran under the road. If the weather was dry I would crawl backwards and forwards through the drain, cobwebs brushing on my face. Sometimes I would hear a car or lorry rumble overhead, sending a shudder down my spine. What if the drain collapsed?

Our salmon harvest would begin at odd hours, again so we could unload at Laxford pier at high tide, and not be left with boxes of dead chilled fish getting less fresh by the minute. Each fish had to be lifted separately out of the cage with a hand net, into a killing box, where it was given a sharp blow on the back of the head and passed to another box, where the packers laid the fish tail to tail, bellies up. The box was then weighed and on one end with a wax crayon was written how many fish it contained, and the full weight. Then it was filled with ice, the lid taped down and the box lifted on to the fishing boat. There was great team spirit and jollity on these days, a feeling of relief, and plans made for future improvements, the hardships of winter forgotten, when the surface of the sea loch freezes over and we would have to break our way through to the cages, one rowing and two ice-breaking in front of the boat.

Once, while my parents had their hands full lifting nets, Dad told me to row back to the fishing boat, some eighty metres away, to pick up the boat hook. It was hard to get a grip with the oars and each time I tried to dig them in and pulled, they slid across the surface of the broken ice. I built myself into a huge rage, tears streaming down my cheeks with frustration. Surely I could do it. After much shouting of parental advice and words of abuse from me, I reached the moored boat. The return journey seemed a little easier, I had new found super strength.

In winter, I did not go to the cages on my own, the water being so cold that if I fell in, I would probably not survive. One windy day, the sea was choppy, and the cages were wet with constant waves breaking on the windward side. I was left to tie the boat up, while Dad fetched the buckets of feed. As we started to feed the fish, I suddenly noticed the boat's painter falling into the water. My knot had come undone. I rushed to the side of the cage, and tried to grab the end but it was too late. Dad was not impressed. He had to strip off his oilskins, heavy jumper and wellies and dive in after the boat. I watched, helpless and sobbing. He was going to be so cross with me when he got back to the cages. Without many words, I sat in the back of the rescued boat, sobbing louder and louder, as Dad rowed to the shore in his dripping shirt and trousers. He was cross, but saw by my distraught sobbing that I had learnt my lesson well. I never let the boat drift away again.

From minor incidents such as this, I learnt to pay attention to detail early on. One small error in bad weather can lead to loss of equipment or, worse, your own life. I have seen things go wrong, and have become so aware of what can go wrong, particularly at sea, that I feel slightly nervous most of the time. This uneasiness keeps me alert. Over-confidence and complacency must be the most dangerous things to any human being. We are kept alive by such a slender thread. What is all around us is more powerful than we can control. We must show great respect to the elements, and use them to our advantage, or when they allow, but to believe we can conquer them can only end in disaster. We can survive extreme conditions, but only by experience and careful thought.

Having been born a woman, I have been blessed with the female sense of survival. Fear may be felt more readily and over-confidence does not show its ugly head as often. There is not the same ego present in me as there seems to be in many males. Perhaps women are more down to earth, more inclined to get on and go for the goal, than make a great song and dance about it. For the survival of the species, many females are necessary, but only a few males. Perhaps they realise instinctively they are more expendable, and that is why they fight each other for supremacy.

4

A World Away

At the age of eleven every child in the far north-west of Scotland has to go away to school. From the small primary schools dotted along the coast, they leave their homes to board weekly on the east coast at the large secondary schools of Dornoch and Golspie. It was 1977. Mum and Dad were getting *English Rose VI* ready to enter the Whitbread Round the World Race with a crew of Adventure School instructors, so plans for my education were also being made. As they would be away for eight months, it was decided that this was as good a time as any to send me to boarding school.

My maternal grandmother came to have a major role in my upbringing at this point, as I somehow passed the entrance exam to a girls' boarding school for the daughters of the clergy in Brighton where Gran lived in a Regency house on the sea front, facing constant problems with her tenants. Whilst a glamorous young Irish woman, she had met her husband on board a ship bound for India and they had married out there. She survived torpedoing on the way back to Britain during the Second World War and he survived the RAF. Mum was born, the fourth child, at the end of the war.

Needless to say, Gran was extremely worried about her daughter, whom she thought worked far too hard, and her small granddaughter who was too skinny. After one of her early visits to Ardmore she returned to London with a whisky bottle full of the well-water we drank and used for everything in the house, and sent a sample to a laboratory to have it tested. The report came back with the question, "Where *is* this water supply?" Traces of whisky had been found in it.

I can remember Gran from an early age, always so well dressed and tall and slim. When she came to stay at Ardmore, she tidied Mum's kitchen cupboards, lining them with newspaper, and did some gardening. She taught me to play cards, as she was a keen bridge player. At home she went to the hairdresser's once a week. When she came to stay with us, she would do her own hair, drying it on rollers with her head in the Rayburn. It had been drilled into her that it was always important to look your best, and she continually checked that she still had lipstick on. I gave Gran facials, covering her skin with cream and rubbing it round and round her face with my bony little fingers, removing the excess with cotton wool. Then I would do her hair. I never quite got the hang of backcombing and directing the hairspray, so concentrated on poking the handle of the comb into her hair, which she liked best.

During my boarding-school years Gran was my mainstay. At first I was stunned by this new way of life, and could not see how I would survive it for the foreseeable future – ten to eighteen seems like for ever when you are just ten. I can only remember the first term through a haze of tears. Everything was so new and alarming, so many people filling the corridors with noise between lessons, heading in the direction of their next class as if programmed. "Tuck" and "mufti" were things I had not come across before. I found it all most strange. So many rules, like only being allowed to wash our hair on Saturdays, being punished for talking after lights-out, trying to sneak bubblegum back in after exeat weekends and being caught stealing hard green pears from over the orphanage wall at the end of the games field. I must have been one of those pathetic children whom teachers hope will snap out of it. I had little or no self-confidence and, although my schoolwork in the subjects I had studied was up to standard, I did not answer questions or read aloud in class unless I had to.

As time went on, I became less homesick, though I did not show potential at anything except taking messages to other classrooms during lessons. As I was always being reprimanded for running in the corridor between classes, teachers knew that I would get the message to the right place and fast.

Every week of these eight years, I received a letter from my father. I insisted on them being typewritten, as his writing is rather difficult to decipher. He would fill a piece of A5 headed writing paper with news and encouragement, beginning the letter with "What ho old top", "Hi Bec", "Dear Cuckoo", "What ho old trout" or some such. He often corrected me on my spelling or grammar first, then went into the news and finally plans for the next holidays. The letters were always in small brown envelopes, and read avidly by my friends! I think they thought Dad was rather strange, although not many of them ever met him. He never came to school, just on the bus to an "away" lacrosse match once! He was rather frightened of teachers and schools.

Being a slow learner, poor at spelling, lacking concentration and not interested in academic subjects, my schoolwork slipped. I failed many more exams than I passed and was advised to study Classical Civilisation rather than Latin at eleven, this being the yardstick between being "thick" or "brainy". However, at the end of the second year, when I was twelve, I was awarded a cup for "Effort and Improvement" in games. I was amazed. So were my family. It was the first thing I had won. My confidence was boosted, and I began to see that there might be some hope. My grandmother pumped more and more Minadex, cod-liver oil and malt into me, in the hope that this would strengthen me and ward off colds, and at fourteen it was decided that I should have my tonsils out, as they had been poisoning me for some time. I missed the school trip to Paris, but became stronger and fitter.

The value of life hit our class in the fourth year. Catherine Gygax, a day girl from Worthing, who was bright and mature for her age, developed cancer. She began chemotherapy and we watched our friend in horror as she became pale and lost the glossy long brown hair she was so proud of and was always brushing. She was no longer able to take part in games lessons, but could still swim. Waiting for the next lesson to begin, still tasting chlorine in the back of our throats, some of us would plait our hair back into perfect order while others, like me, waited for the tangles to dry. Catherine brushed her hair with a soft brush, but handfuls came out with every stroke. Her eyes filled with tears, no one knew what to say. She turned to a close friend and laughed, crying at the same time. She had her hair cut short, and a wig was made out of the cut hair. Catherine struggled on bravely. Days of school were missed and her diet was changed to vegetarian. The cancer seemed to abate after a year or so of treatment, but soon after we left after our fifth year it came back with a vengeance. Her family were told before Christmas that there was little time left. They chose not to tell her. Shortly after New Year she died at the age of just sixteen. I did not think life would be quite the same again, being close to this tragedy. Everything in life, I realised, must be done to the full, it must all be made worthwhile. Every now and again, I need reminders of this to jerk me back into reality. An expedition which brings you back to the basics of life and day-to-day survival is just the medicine for this.

I spent my last two years of schooling in the sixth form at Gordonstoun. Its morning run and cold-shower image fitted well with my upbringing and I loved my time there. "*Plus est en Vous*", the school motto, was certainly put into practice. Everyone was given the chance to be in the choir or a play. Even if you had no talent or experience, a small part could always be found. I had auditioned for a production of *Oliver* when I was thirteen, and not even been allowed to be in the chorus – how damning to feel you are useless at this early age.

In my second term, I showed prospective pupils and their parents round the school. If David Bowie's child had been a daughter I would have had a celebrity to show around. Instead, I had to lurk behind hedges and position myself in front of the library door to get a good look at him. The main school duty I held was Captain of Grounds. I was poor at this, keen to pick up rubbish myself after my father's fanatical line on the subject, but lacking the confidence to get others to do so as well. I was so ineffective that the Deputy Head threatened me with having to give a talk in Chapel on "rubbish".

Saturday afternoons during the first and second terms were often spent watching Rugby matches. Boys were a new discovery at Gordonstoun. We stood along the touchlines cheering on our favoured young men, often freezing in impractical clothing we hoped was creating the right impression. I went through the usual sequence of short romances, and the most serious one ended with my young man being expelled a few days before my 'A'-level exams began for shooting a fat boy climbing a ladder in the backside with an air gun. Exit Robert. He sent me a bunch of red roses for my eighteenth birthday, and I met up with him as soon as school ended. We said goodbye in a Tube station in London, as I had to go back to work at the Gordonstoun International Summer School for a month. I had seen this type of farewell in films and had wished it was me, but when it really did happen, I wished it was not. It was much more painful than I had imagined and strangers stared at my tear-streaked face. The next time I saw Robert it was not the same.

When I started at Gordonstoun, Dad and the skipper of *English Rose VI*, Andy Briggs, had set off on a non-stop round-the-world sailing trip.

They hoped to be the fastest boat ever to do this without resupply. Dad was forty-five, and thought this a good time to put his life into perspective. "O hear us when we cry to thee For those in peril on the sea" brought many the tear to my eye during the long months they were away. There were weeks when Mum heard nothing.

At the end of the spring term was the school cross-country running competition. I had been running for a couple of years during the holidays, and was really keen, but at school I had not done a lot of training. I ran along the cliffs with the boys once a week, being left behind, but building up the distance. It paid off, and I won the girls' competition. Dad was nearing Britain by this time, and could speak to Mum on the ship-to-shore radio. He was thrilled to learn I had won. We had run a lot together, me always being left behind, but now I was catching up!

Part Two
PERU

5

Elizabeth

Our family holidays were always a test of what one was made of. Perhaps everybody's are. But we did seem to develop a habit of taking things increasingly to the extreme.

With the Adventure School occupying the summer months, holidays had to happen after September and the lure of somewhere warm to set us up for the rest of the galeswept Sutherland winter would be irresistible. Not that warmth meant lying in deckchairs on distant sunny beaches. Far from it.

My parents tended to use the stages of my youthful career as an excuse for special holidays. Before I went away to school at Kinlochbervie at the age of seven they took me on a cruise aboard *English Rose V*, a Nicholson 32-foot, without engine. It was a winter cruise down the North Atlantic to the Azores and the Cape Verde Islands via the Spanish Sahara. On the way home we were swamped by a huge wave in a Force Nine in the Minch, only managing to stay afloat by bailing with buckets and pans.

When I left Gordonstoun at eighteen with two 'A'-levels and no idea what I wanted to do, we planned another family holiday. Dad favoured the Himalayas, but Mum and I outvoted him. We wanted to go to Peru. We could try and track down his old friend Elvin Berg who fifteen years before had guided Dad's team down the most dangerous part of the Amazon where it first becomes navigable. The Bergs, originally from Norway, had grown in Dad's memory as an ideal rural community displaying all the virtues of self-reliance and good husbandry. They lived a Swiss Family Robinson-style existence deep in the jungle, five days' walk from the nearest dirt track. The parallels with Ardmore were obvious. In my mind's eye I could see us stepping carefully through an emerald jungle alive with the cries of monkeys and the screech of brilliant parrots, with the odd deadly snake entwined in the branches just above our heads like a deodorant commercial.

My view was entirely derived from a childhood playing Rafting-down-the-Amanoz with Dad in my parents' bed while Mum dressed and made breakfast on the rare days they allowed themselves a lie-in. The game started with building our raft. We would cut large trees down with axes, "chop-chop, chop-chop, nnyaw crash!" until we had enough for the raft, then we would "tie-tie, tie-tie, tie-tie" and the raft was built. Waving goodbye to the "friendly Indians" who had helped us, we would set off downstream, "paddle-paddle, paddle-paddle", keeping an eye open for alligators and piranha fish. As there were stuffed specimens of these downstairs, I felt pretty confident what to look out for. When nightfall came, we would tie up to the bank and begin fishing. Dad would tie the line to his big toe while I got the frying pan ready to take the catch. Tremendous struggles with big fish would ensue, but once on the raft they would go swiftly into my pan, "sizzle-sizzle, sizzle-sizzle". Exhausted from our exciting day of adventure we would lie down to sleep, but invariably, soon after Dad started his snoring impressions, "unfriendly Indians" would begin shooting poisonous arrows at us from upstream, and we would have to paddle on in a frenzy of terror to safe waters. Sometimes the game would begin again, if there was time, or we would go and have breakfast. The Amazon must be like this.

Which was perhaps why Dad did not think that the three of us would be a strong enough team, so asked two of the School's instructors to come with us. Justin Matterson and Edward Ley-Wilson were both keen, young and fit and jumped at the chance. While we were having our injections and assembling our kit, Dad telephoned a Franciscan Mission he knew of in Sussex to see if they still had people out in Peru, and wanted any mail taken out to them. "Oh, haven't you heard? We had to close the Mission with all the trouble out there," came the reply. "What trouble?" Dad asked. The broad outline of a desperate terrorist war was poured out as Dad listened in horror. None of this news had been reported in Britain, as after the first and second mass murders by the Sendero Luminoso guerrillas, no one was interested. What sort of a family holiday would this be for his wife and eighteen-year-old daughter? We were too close to departure to get any refund on the five air tickets. I suppose we could have adjusted our plans, been good tourists following the well-trodden Inca Trail and come home. But that was not my father's style and, anyway, he now wanted to find out how his old friend and inspiration Elvin Berg was surviving the troubles. So we set off for our holiday in the war zone. For me it was finishing-school Ridgway-style. It proved to be the start of a lot more.

Contemplating our revised scenario I knew that I had a real sense of adventure. I felt frightened, but at the same time could not wait to see what would unfold. In Lima the British Embassy advised us not to go into the area we proposed, which had been declared a *Zona Rocha* or Red Zone. It was made clear to us that if we did not return by the date we specified, no one would be sent to look for us. Thus warned, and armed with a clutch of poorly typed but elaborately rubber-stamped letters from every possible authority we could get to see, we set off.

Osambre, the Bergs' jungle farm was our goal. If these reports of terror were true, we would need to be a strong team to survive. So we walked for a month at high altitude to get fit and used to the hard routine. On a diet of potatoes, bought from desperately poor peasants, we began at one of the sources of the Amazon at approximately 14,500 feet. We were following the Apurimac, the Great Speaker, the Amazon's longest tributary and Dad's route of fifteen years before. Several dramatic learning experiences occurred during this training phase, all tinged with varying degrees of altitude sickness.

Unfriendly locals tried to burn us out of our camp on the first night, then I was mistaken for a nurse, so did my best to clean up a young man who had had his head beaten in with rocks until he gave his few cigarettes to his attackers. He had a rather ominous bubble sticking out of his skull, which his fellow Indians had no worry about bursting. However, after a night's rest he set off, seemingly none the worse, into the hills. After this Dad lent me his favourite hunting knife and gave me instructions on what to do if attacked by bandits on horseback. I had to ram the knife into the horse's chest. Luckily Dad's much prized weapon never had to graduate from a vegetable knife.

Ed and I both suffered from bad colds, mine resulting in otitis media, an infection of the inner ear causing pressure and excruciating pain, until the eardrum bursts and the pressure equalises. Somehow, intense pain in the head always seems more worrying than in other parts of the body; it was so bad, I just wanted to die. But once the eardrum burst and the pain was relieved I was only deaf for a couple of weeks. I had been lucky in a country where life is cheap. We returned to Cuzco for a few days' rest, leaner, fitter and a team, before heading into the *Zona Rocha* to our real goal.

After being lost for twenty-four hours with no water, on a steep spur covered with scrubby jungle and tarantulas, we eventually got down to the muddy, tumbling Apurimac, swelling every day with the start of the rainy season. There was no way to cross, the river forming a natural boundary. Justin was a keen swimmer and thought he could make it. We watched helplessly as the Great Speaker swallowed Justin, then spat him out on a rocky beach further downstream. The coca farmers on the other side were so impressed by this bravery that they built a raft and helped us across. They then had the problem of what to do with us. We could be terrorist sympathisers, arms or cocaine dealers. Frightened for their own lives, they route-marched us for a night and then three days to see the military commandant in charge of the area.

Now only a few days from our goal, we were beginning to hear disturbing rumours. Elvin Berg's farm at Osambre had been attacked the previous year; Elvin had been tortured and burnt alive. It had been the first murder by the Sendero Luminoso on this side of the river. Shocked, bitterly disappointed, exhausted and not allowed to go any further into Sendero country, we were forced by the military to leave for our own safety. Two 14,000-foot mountain passes and at least a four-day walk would get us to the end of a dirt track to catch a truck to safety. We set off with heavy hearts. Our great plan had come to nothing. We could now see that everyone in the area was terrified. It was just a matter of time before they, too, would be attacked by the Senderos. Few had ever seen gringos before, so were often hostile and suspicious. Our retreat was a miserable one.

Dad had a cold and, not wanting to risk him incurring the same problems I had had, we decided to rest for a couple of days in the village of Accobamba on our way up to the first mountain pass. While Dad slept, Mum and I explored the village and were invited in to drink coffee by a young crippled woman who said her name was Birginie. Explaining our visit, we discovered quite by chance that Elvin Berg had a young daughter and that she was actually living in that very village. We were astonished and asked for more details. She was with her maternal grandparents, the Huamans, who were refugees from the Senderos, explained our hostess. What about her mother? Her mother was now elsewhere.

The little girl was five or six years old, the woman told us. Touching her own straight black hair, she said how brown and wavy the child's was, and what beautiful fair skin she had. They called her *La Gringita*, the little white girl. But the family were very afraid, she said, they had been through terrible times. Grandfather Huaman had been *gobernador*, head man, of a village close to Osambre, called Lucmahuayco. When the terrorists attacked, their aim was to kill anyone in authority. He escaped into the jungle and disappeared for over a month, presumed dead. As a reprisal, the Senderos murdered his only son, presenting the boy's mother with her son's bloodied clothes. The village was burnt, Elvin's daughter escaped with her mother, who was profoundly deaf and driven half mad by the atrocities she had witnessed. Together with her grandmother, aunt and two small cousins, they left with what they could. At least they had their lives.

The three Huaman women, determined to survive for their children, fled to Accobamba, a couple of days' walk higher into the mountains. They found an abandoned house and kept alive with the little they had. Weeks later the grandfather emerged from the jungle, emaciated and sick. Now they were trying to acquire a small patch of land to feed themselves and rebuild their shattered lives.

As our Spanish was poor, we had to listen intently and ask for a lot of repetitions before we pieced together the true extent of the horror these innocent people had been through, but in a strange way, it was beginning to feel as if we had been led to this point. We could so easily have walked past the collection of mud houses, brown pin pricks in a steep-sided emerald valley, if Dad had not fallen ill.

He was amazed by the story we unfolded. We must meet the little girl they called Lizbet. That afternoon, Simeona, a thin, gently spoken woman with a shy smile who spoke good Spanish, agreed to take the three of us to meet the family. She told us that the Huamans spoke only Quechua and she would translate, warning us they were very nervous, frightened people.

I will never forget that first meeting. Not much was said, not much could be said, and nothing need be said. I wrote in my diary:

Simeona utters a few words in Quechua and we smile. The old lady breathes heavily, her eyes filled with fear, she disappears into the room on her left and returns with three grey-looking sheepskins, she lays them on a rough bench along the right-hand wall of the alcove and signals for us to sit down. Three grubby children sit on sheepskins on the floor eating watery soup from chipped enamel bowls. They and a young woman stop, only their eyes move, as if frozen with fear. Lizbet is the oldest child. Dad says, "That's Elvin," as soon as he sees the daughter of his friend. We sit and look at each other, Simeona breaks the ice by explaining that we are friends of Elvin Berg and mean no harm. They continue to look worried. The smallest child cries and is immediately picked up by its mother, the other two begin to eat ravenously again. Lizbet wears a crochet yellow and white hat pulled tightly down, a deep-pink knitted dress and blue tracksuit bottoms with blackened feet below. Her skin is a lot paler than the others, and her hair is slightly less blue-black. For us it is a very emotional time.

Lizbet continued to eat, she did everything slowly and precisely, a past master at peeling cooked potatoes and a highly treasured egg. All the while she peeped up at us from under her hat, but remained quiet and composed. I asked if I could take some photographs for the distant relatives back in Norway. Lizbet's grandmother said I could, but they wanted to smarten themselves up. I managed to take a few before any smartening had been done, and through the smartening process, which threw the family into a turmoil of excitement, rummaging through bags of clothes for their best kit. Still the centre of our attention remained composed and unruffled. She had her face washed with cold water from a gourd, her hair wetted and combed and a clean green knitted dress put on. The other two children and the two women communicated, but Lizbet remained silent all the time; there was a look of great sadness in her eyes, she almost seemed removed from her surroundings.

We wanted to give the child something to remember this meeting by in memory of her father. I took off my confirmation chain and Mum slid a thin silver ring from her finger. It had belonged to her grand-mother, who was also called Elizabeth. We put the ring on the chain and Mum placed it over the child's head. I had to choke back my tears.

We got up to go. We did not want to worry the old lady any more. This chance meeting had affected us all. Lizbet's grandmother walked towards Mum, held her hands tightly and looked into her eyes, before they hugged each other. I wanted to get away, I was already crying. Why was life so cruel to these innocent people? That child had been through more in her six short years than most go through in sixty.

As we left, Lizbet walked towards Dad, and bravely said, "Ciao, Pappi." Children and adults commonly refer to men as Pappi in Quechua, but maybe this white man reminded her of the father she had seen so little of. As I walked slowly ahead of Mum, Dad and Simeona, my mind was racing. Tears now flooded down my cheeks. What could we do to help this poor child?

Simeona continued to fill in the facts. Lizbet's mother was away working, the child was pining for her. With not enough food to go round, no father and being looked after by elderly grandparents, there was little future for her. Simeona hesitated slightly, then said, "The grandmother has asked if you would take Lizbet home with you."

My heart leapt. I had always wanted a brother or sister, and knew Mum would have liked more children. Dad's view, however, was that most of the problems in the world were caused by too many people, so if he only had one child, he would not be adding to them. But this small child already existed . . . Had the whole trip been leading to this point in some form of destiny for us three? The coincidences that had led us to this meeting certainly could not have been pre-planned, even with Dad's meticulous plans.

In my mind there was no doubt as to what we should do, but it was really up to Mum and Dad. It was they who would have to continue to give up their freedom with another young child, they who would have to pay the bills. There might also be all sorts of emotional and psychological problems to deal with. Lizbet might not find it possible to love us or, worse, we might not find it possible to love her.

But what would be the consequences of leaving her behind? Surely anything was better than starving or being murdered and, as her grandfather kept saying later in the evening when he had returned from the field, "*Opitunidad*." Such opportunities would be open to her.

The non-stop sailing trip round the world had certainly softened Dad – I could not imagine him even considering another child before. He had admired Elvin, and expressed the hope that if the situation had been reversed, Elvin would have looked after me. (That would have been an interesting, different life!) Also, having been adopted himself, I think he felt that he would be able to relate to the sort of problems Lizbet might encounter. So there never needed to be a lot of discussion between us. Our minds were made up. If the family wanted us to take Lizbet to be part of our family, we would. It was up to them. Justin and Ed could not believe their ears when we told them what had happened during the day, and what we had decided to do.

After some formal discussion with Lizbet's grandfather, conducted through Cesar, the resident teacher, who came from Cuzco and spoke English, Spanish and Quechua, things seemed to be decided. Lizbet sat cross-legged on a sheepskin, peeping up at her grandfather every so often, and he looked down at her lovingly.

Juan Huaman would come with us to see Lizbet's mother, who helped in the house of a cousin at the end of the road where we had to go to catch the truck. If she agreed, Lizbet would go with us. But, he explained, he could not leave the village for three days until after a community meeting at which he hoped to be allotted some land. We agreed to wait.

It was now dark and Juan urged us to go straight back to the school where we were staying, as the men of the village guard, the Ronda, might mistake us for terrorists. We slept in our clothes for those three nights, ready to run into the jungle with the rest of the people as soon as we heard a warning shot. When one came we were at the door in a flash but it was a false alarm. A Ronda rifle had gone off by accident, taking the barrel with it, and these were the best weapons they had. Some men were only armed with sharpened sticks.

We visited Lizbet's family each day and I was already dreaming all sorts of dreams about introducing a new little sister to Ardmore. But the three days were also enough for her grandfather to have second thoughts and by the morning of departure he had changed his mind about letting us take her with us. I was confused and upset. Lizbet's grandmother started to take the chain with the ring on it off her granddaughter's neck, but we insisted she keep it. The walk-out was terrible. It poured, my bites itched, there was nothing left to say, the people in the villages through which we passed were suspicious and hostile. With good reason. On the second day word came that the terrorists had taken a nearby village. Everyone was on the move, trying to get out of harm's way.

At the end of the third day we found ourselves walking with Juan Huaman and his family and he told us that he was willing for us to adopt Lizbet after all, but he must talk to her mother first. So we went with him to Huancacalle, a dreadful slummy village which had grown as a market at the end of the dirt road. Lizbet's mother was there. We let them spend some time alone before presenting ourselves at a large, well-looked-after mud house. Lizbet's mother, Leocadia, came out of the house, smiling, and was guided towards us. Dad showed her the photograph of Elvin in his book, *Amazon Journey*. She continued to smile. She was gentle and childlike, how much of this could she really understand? It seemed as if she had to be guided everywhere, so how could she look after her child if anything happened to her parents? Our truck was to leave in ten minutes. It was agreed that if they decided they did want us to adopt Lizbet, they must get her to Lima with all the completed documents. We would do everything from there.

Returning to Britain in mid-December for Christmas was like entering a different world. Lizbet was strong in all our thoughts and what we had seen and been through in her desperate country had had a profound effect on us all. It left me with little patience to settle down to the intensive secretarial course I had asked Gran to line up for me in London. Early one morning in May, the telephone rang. It could only be my father ringing this early. I tried to sound awake as I answered with my eyes still closed.

"Lizbet is in Cuzco with Nick and Igor Asheshov – so it looks like you will have a little sister after all."

My heart leapt and I was suddenly awake.

Nick Asheshov, half-English half-Russian journalist, was the brother of Anna Asheshov who had been on Dad's 1970 expedition. He had helped at the Lima end of that trip and our recent one. Igor was his son. As soon as the rainy season ended, Nick and Igor had flown to Cuzco and taken the train to Quillabamba where they visited Padre Santiago, the Franciscan Father who had baptised Lizbet and helped them pick up the threads which led to the signing of the adoption papers and the day Lizbet was lifted up on to a horse in front of Igor and set out on the biggest adventure of her young life. She didn't utter a squeak for days. Only when she saw the bright lights of Quillabamba did she begin to react.

Nick and Igor took Lizbet to Lima, where she stayed with them while the myriad of adoption papers went through on both sides. It was not until October that Dad finally got entry clearance for her to come to Scotland. When Lizbet came out of the jungle, she was nearly seven years old, weighed thirty-nine pounds and was three feet six inches tall. She had chronic malnutrition, from which her liver and heart will never recover, a tapeworm in her stomach and head lice. Most of her teeth were black stumps and so tender that she would not open her mouth for the dentist but had to be put under general anaesthetic to remove them.

I completed my secretarial course and returned to Ardmore to help during the summer and autumn. I wanted to be there when Lizbet arrived, to be a sister for her, so that she could get an idea of what it was like to be a child of our parents. Most of all, I wanted to make her settling-in as easy as possible.

Lizbet flew from Lima to London and on to Inverness with Nick and Igor in October 1986, a year after we had begun our travels. We were all anxious about this meeting. What if Elizabeth was an emotional wreck? She might cry all the time, she might be violent and aggressive, she might not like us. I was pretty sure that we could all love her, but we would not know for sure until we got to know each other. They arrived at Portlevorchy, the lone grey stone croft on the other side of the loch, just as dusk was darkening the sky. Dad stayed on board the fishing boat, while Mum and I rowed ashore to meet them. Quite a different little person, seemingly full of confidence, appeared like a gem through the grey light. Dressed in a bright red skirt, white blouse and black waistcoat seen in a fairytale book in Lima, "the Inca Princess", as my grandmother later named her, greeted us as if she had always known us. I wondered if she really did remember our meeting the year before.

Lizbet was almost unrecognisable. Her proper name was Elizabeth, she soon became Isso. Her eyes were bright, her hair was cut into a thick and glossy bob, and she looked strong. The sad, lost expression had gone. Everything was new and exciting. She was a survivor, but underneath this tough exterior still lurked a frightened little girl who needed lots of love, constant reassurance and stability.

The first night all my worries were put to rest. I just knew that it was right. Putting her to bed, Mum and I discovered that around her neck she still wore my confirmation chain and Mum's ring, kept hidden under her blouse, in case anyone should try to take them from her. Her fingernails were terribly bitten and the scars from early mosquito bites still remained. But she was the same little girl. Elvin's daughter.

Elizabeth

People have asked if I felt jealous of the new member of our family, but I can honestly say that I have never felt jealous of her or of the attention she has received from the rest of our family. I love her as if she were of my own blood. She has given me so much.

Life seemed to continue almost as normal. We did not speak a common language, but most day-to-day things could be understood easily. After a while I began to take Elizabeth to Kinlochbervie school two mornings a week to the same teacher and the same tiny desks that I had sat at. Elizabeth called me Ribeeka and held on to me tightly. She dared not say a word at school, just peeping up now and then at the other children, who were wonderful and welcoming. We used to stay for lunch, where she always got her money's worth, eating as if every meal could be her last. Malnutrition is hard to forget, and she was expending a lot of nervous energy. Elizabeth still ate the jungle way, knives and forks really were not necessary. She delicately tore the chicken from the bone then proceeded to crunch away at the bone to get any remaining goodness – I am glad to say that she still does this six years later.

I felt so protective towards this small child, who was by no means always good. She tested us continually and we had great battles, for, despite all that happened to her, her temperament is still bright and strong.

Elizabeth graduated from these early learning stages to going to school each day on her own, walking in and out along the track morning and evening. She grew from being a little dolly to quite a young lady, as if in the blink of an eye. At the age of eleven, and still some way behind in her learning, she had to begin boarding school, as I had. She now attends an ideal school, where there are just twelve pupils who, for various reasons, have missed out on part of their education. They learn in a practical manner and are gaining confidence daily. Elizabeth truly loves school.

The love that I have seen between Elizabeth and my mother is remarkable. If they did not look so different you would think they were natural mother and daughter. It seems as if they have always been together. Elizabeth has made our lives richer, I love her as my sister. Some things are meant to be and this was one of them.

6

Return to the Altiplano

During the summer of 1989 Dad decided to go back to Peru. The situation there had become much worse than it was in 1985. Then Alan Garcia had just been elected president and there was great hope that he would be able to bring the country under control. Now he dared not show his face in public, while the Sendero Luminoso controlled an increasingly large area. We felt it was important to return to Peru to get word to Elizabeth's family, if they were still alive, of her well-being and progress since she left Accobamba. We also wanted to find out for her as much as possible about the paternal side of her family.

Dad asked Mum if she wanted to go with him, but they both knew her first duty now lay at home with Elizabeth. So he asked me – in passing at first, to give me time to let the idea sink in. I am not one to make hasty decisions, and I needed time to think about this trip. I knew the possible dangers and that my relations, particularly my grandmother, would do all they could to persuade me from another death-defying trip with my father.

But much had happened in the four years since we had discovered Elizabeth. I was now twenty-two years old and had been working at Ardmore for three years. The friendship that had built up between Justin and me on our previous trip to Peru had turned into something stronger and, much to Dad's concern, we had fallen in love. But Justin had been the chief instructor and skipper of *English Rose VI* for three years, and it was time for him to move on to other challenges. He had decided to run two thousand miles along the Himalayas in under a hundred days with Ed Ley-Wilson, who had also been with us on the previous trip to Peru. So he was beginning to concentrate on training for this. These sorts of challenges seemed to come to us naturally. We had spent a month cycling in the Atlas Mountains in Morocco in 1987,

and ran the New York Marathon in 1988. It was just the way I had
been brought up – there was not a lot of sitting on beaches or staying
in nice hotels. Which was why I found the idea of going back to Peru
so tempting. It would be living life to the full.

I was running our International Summer School, with up to sixty
young people aged between twelve and eighteen and eight instructors
to co-ordinate each day. How many of these would pass up an opportunity like this? The thought of the trip nagged at me. I was always one
to give it a go, but I remembered how ill I had been in 1985. I did not
want to let anyone down. Surely I was physically stronger now, doing
the five-mile morning run faster than I had ever before. I had learnt to
cope with discomfort over the past three years of working at Ardmore,
and being the only girl instructor had taught me that in most things I
was just as able as the boys. One of Dad's favourite aphorisms kept
coming back to me: if faced with two opportunities, always choose the
bolder.

My mind was fairly made up, but I needed to discuss it with Mum.

"If I were you, I would go like a shot, but we both know it will
be very dangerous and really perhaps I, as your mother, shouldn't be
encouraging you."

I would go, I couldn't miss an opportunity like this. Of course it was
going to be dangerous, but this time I would be prepared. I felt fitter
and stronger than ever before, and as long as we had a fair chance, I
knew I could cope.

Dad hoped that Igor Asheshov would come with us. In typical Peruvian style, it was almost impossible to track Igor down from this country,
but he was to prove invaluable to our success. Malcolm Sutherland, a
twenty-year-old instructor, who was to take his Regular Commissions
Board examination to join the Army early the next spring, also joined
the team. His height and strength belied his gentle nature.

As the date of departure drew nearer, plans developed. We would go
into the jungle to try and find Elizabeth's uncle, Olaf Berg, then to
Accobamba to see Elizabeth's maternal family, taking a hearing aid to
Elizabeth's mother. Olaf was the only Berg still alive and had been at
Osambre the day Elvin was murdered. We must find out as much as
possible about Elizabeth's family while we still could, so that, when she
asked, she had the opportunity to be told everything. There should be
no secrets from an adopted child.

Just before we were to fly, an article about our trip was published in the *Daily Telegraph*, which ended excitedly:

John discovered the identity of the man who killed Elvin – a leading terrorist called Orrosco who habitually camps beside the rivers and, if surprised, escapes by leaping into the water. The task of tracking him down, in jungle infested with fanatical revolutionaries, would daunt lesser men, but Ridgway is not easily deflected, and is now hell-bent on bringing the murderer to justice.

Though not strictly true, it was the stuff that sold newspapers. Gran bought one and was in a terrible state, and my uncle, Under-Secretary General in charge of the UN Peacekeeping Forces, wrote, "We beg you not to go, John, at least don't take Rebecca."

All my doubts surged back. Was it worth the risks? I did not want to upset my family, but with Mum still supporting me, after much deliberation, I decided that I would go.

The flight to Lima was extremely empty, there were very few tourists in Lima and Cuzco. Maybe I had after all made the wrong decision? We travelled to the remote village of Yupanca by train, then truck. We would be walking from here.

The smell of paraffin and soap hit me as I entered the shop. It was some five seconds before my eyes became accustomed to the darkness. A few last items must be purchased before leaving Yupanca and as a treat for the first few days of walking, which are always the worst, I bought some rather poor-looking oranges, deliciously juicy but often sour, and with an occasional worm for nourishment. Next was a small plastic bag of undersized garlic bulbs to flavour the stodge of rice served at every meal, and if we were lucky the vegetables or fish to go with it. I bought a roll of thin, hard, pink loo paper for Dad, who'd been borrowing mine for the past week; things like this begin to niggle after a while, and a precious roll of Andrex becomes a real luxury and the most important thing amongst your kit when you get the inevitable diarrhoea.

Igor suggested we buy a large bag of coca leaves to encourage the two muleteers, Roberto and Simeon, as well as grumpy old Don Pancho, Olaf's uncle and our guide, who was all in favour of something for nothing. I also bought fifteen flat, hard bread rolls: these were comparatively expensive because there was a flour shortage in Peru, and bread in this area was made with flour smuggled across the border from Chile. Getting used to the local food on any trip is something I have to set my mind to. Bread would be the easiest thing to eat, but the taste of these rolls made my stomach turn.

The last item on the list was a torch for Roberto, Simeon and Don Pancho, who insisted they needed it to keep night watch on the horses and protect them from the mighty jaguar, well known for stealing any size of animal during the night. We were a bit sceptical about these tales, taking them as just a good excuse for acquiring a torch to show off to others who did not have one!

At last the three horses were loaded and I said goodbye to the crowd of little girls who'd gathered around to look at the gringa. They whispered to each other behind dirty cupped hands. Keeping their dark and glinting almond eyes fixed on me, they pointed out how strange I looked: how tall I was, what fair skin I had, the silver ring on my finger and thin silver bracelet on my wrist, the four ear-rings I wore in one ear, and my blue eyes. But most fascinating of all was my fair hair, which they had only seen on the faded old Coca-cola adverts. They all wanted to touch it, and often called me "*el zorra*", the vixen; mountain foxes are silver grey, the closest-colour animal fur to my hair.

My feelings about these children had changed since 1985. I never liked the way they talked and pointed at me but after living with Elizabeth for three years, I felt I understood. There was little else for them to do, their lives were so monotonous, and we looked so strange.

Don Pancho's son, Raoul Beingolea, wore his fine new hat to see us off and raised it as he shook our hands one by one, wishing us the best of luck with our journey – formal introductions and farewells were typical of Raoul. I had come to realise his position was tragic. His family had lost all their land in the Agrarian Reform. Now he was running for mayor, a brave undertaking, as the Senderos were killing all the mayors they could find. I suspected that this physically small man wanted to be a big man, and this he would become if he was voted mayor.

The path was narrow, clinging to the steep valley side, like the sheep tracks at home. Looking around I could see a sea of deep-green rainforest stretching on for ever in all directions. Spurs from the sierra reached down into the valley like bony fingers from a green hand groping out for something unknown. Except for the path we walked on, there was no sign that man existed.

Walking behind Dad, I could see the first beads of sweat soaking through his blue shirt, the back of his neck glistened, and his short hair was starting to stick together under his floppy old hat. I wondered how many miles I had walked following those army-boot prints and big splayed feet in the Sutherland mountains and Peruvian Andes. In 1985 we had walked in a special order. Dad was first, keeping the pace and finding the way, I was second to keep my morale high, Mum third so she could chat to everyone, Ed came fourth and Justin fifth, to check no one fell off the back. Keeping morale high is the most important thing, and the weakest always needs to be near the front.

I could feel the gentle prickle of sweat on my forehead, just below my hat. This was also an old faithful, a man's hat, as Peruvians are smaller than us. I didn't want to lose this vital piece of kit in the wind, so I had sewn the ends of a multi-coloured boot lace into the hat just above my ears to hang on a loop below my chin. With the remains of the boot lace, I made a pair of cufflinks for Dad; back in Cuzco and Lima weeks later, they were greatly admired. Maybe we set a new trend for fashion-conscious Peruvian men!

Way above a racing torrentina we stopped where a small stream crossed the path, while the horses drank. Don Pancho arrived in his ancient white wellies and lit another fag, still wheezing and panting from the climb; I think he was surprised the overweight señor and the weedy-looking señorita had managed to keep going this far. Malc handed round the last of the boiled sweets he had bought at Heathrow. There wasn't much chat, I think we were all too full of anticipation to say anything.

Don Pancho now disappeared ahead, belying his sixty-eight years, in a series of short cuts which we weren't fast enough to follow. Coming to a place where the scrub had been cleared away exposing the dark fertile soil, we saw a tangle of children looking down at us in stunned silence. Although still only an hour's walk from the road end, I doubt they had seen gringos before.

The flora and landscape began to change as we climbed higher. Tropical vegetation faded into washed-out yellowy-green icchu grass. The stunted trees were covered with thorns and entwined together; many different pathways twisted and turned through this maze and it was easy to get lost. The horses had got well ahead. They were on a grassy slope on the far side of the valley. Don Pancho didn't seem to care about us much, just wanting to get far enough ahead of us to sit down and have another fag while he waited! The heat was starting to get to Dad, and I could see he was going to be cross with Don Pancho for not staying to show us the way. From above we heard the voices of Roberto and Simeon shouting to us to walk higher. At last the ground levelled out a bit, more like pasture, and we gained on the horses. Ahead lay a small thatched mud house, surrounded by a field dug for potatoes, and a grey stone wall; the only sign of life was a small flock of sheep, straggling high up on the hill. There was so much in this way of sub- sistence living similar to that of the Highland crofter, but in Scotland the people were vanishing to the cities, tempted by better-paid jobs. Here they were fleeing for their lives before the ever-encroaching terrorists.

When we stopped for lunch Dad asked how many hours it would take to get to Pampaconas. Don Pancho said it would take us about six, maybe more; we might not make it before nightfall. My heart sank. I remembered Raoul telling us it would only take half a day to get to Pampaconas, so this meant that all the walking times between villages that he had given us would have to be doubled at least.

This bad news got us moving straight away. Roberto stopped here and there at the odd house to stick up "Vote Beingolea" posters for Raoul who had provided him with a tin of glue and an old glued-up brush. I doubted if the few passers-by would ever see the promised improvements Raoul talked of; either because his message would be blown away by the harsh altiplano wind or because Raoul would never become mayor – if he was lucky.

The altiplano is a different country from the rainforest a few thousand feet below. The Quechua people themselves are different. Life up there is much harder, the staple diet potatoes, the soil poor. The path became wider and much more rocky now. Dad and I walked a bit more slowly for fear of altitude sickness. We were on the main route out from the ancient Inca Kingdom of the Clouds of Vilcabamba. It had been well trodden over the years by people taking their produce to market, and more recently by families fleeing from the terrorists. In a steep rocky gully we came upon a cave which served as somewhere for travellers to shelter for the night. Many of them had scrawled their names in crayon or charcoal on the bare rock. One word was written large and often:

MALARIA – families listed their names and dates beside it. It was a horrible thought.

Only one day's walk from here and we'd be in terrorist country. Over the past eight years the Senderos had seized control of the jungle and now they were moving up through the rainforest and on to the bleak altiplano. Where and when they would stop, no one knew, but everyone was suspicious and frightened.

The afternoon sun turned to cloud and then fine drizzle. Dad and I put on our green plastic ponchos and continued plodding along in tired silence. My head was really thumping now, and every small rise in the path became more of an effort. Soon we were in thick mist. The daylight was fading fast, along with our energy and patience. Outside Pampaconas, groups of older children appeared through the mist to look us over, but not with shy giggles and smiles. Their laughter was harsh and threatening. The rain was even heavier now, and thunder shook the mud-brick houses in the darkness. Flashes of lightning illuminated Igor's racing figure as he dashed about, negotiating for a dry floor for us to sleep on.

There had been a market and the celebrations were still going on. Through the rain I could see lots of dark faces like moths around the paraffin pressure lamps. Most of the people were drunk by now and we didn't want to get involved in any arguments. The locals would assume we were *Norte Americanos*, who don't usually go down too well with Peruvians. Luckily, the darkness hid us and we avoided confrontation. A man swathed in polythene took us to an open porch out of the rain, where a large Quechua woman dished out bowls of thick mutton stew from a huge pot. I was feeling sick from the altitude, so gave most of my greasy helping to Dad and Malcolm who were only too pleased.

The plan was to walk to a place called Lambras where Antonio Huaman lived with his wife and family. They were friends of both Olaf and Olaf's uncle, Don Pancho, and we hoped we would be able to persuade Antonio to guide us to Capiro, where Olaf was thought to be, as he was about the only person who knew the route through the jungle. Lambras was not marked on our map, but some places had had two or three different names since pre-Inca times. Don Pancho said it would only take half a day to reach Lambras; I hoped he meant half a day at our speed, not the Raoul times of the previous day.

Pampaconas looked rather eerie in the early morning mist, and we

Helping Lance with the hens.

On the run with Dad.

Mrs Ada Bell's Academy, my best chance to be top of the class.

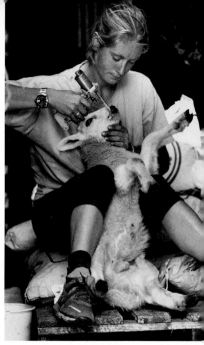

Mum, Dad and I at Ardmore.   Dosing the lambs in June.

Ardmore in the mid-80s, three miles from the road.

Building the raft at Capiro in 1989.
Running the Apurimac rapids with Olaf and rifle.

Juan Huaman and Josephina slaughtered one of their three sheep for us at Accobamba.

My sister Elizabeth, the day we found her in Accobamba, with granny Josephina and cousin Johanny.

Dad and I crunching into delicious fried trout at Toronc.

A spot of winter training in the Tide Race.

Plenty of insulation from the icy rock was needed for a good night's sleep.
An infected cut gave Nigel blood poisoning that jeopardised his life and our safety on the water.

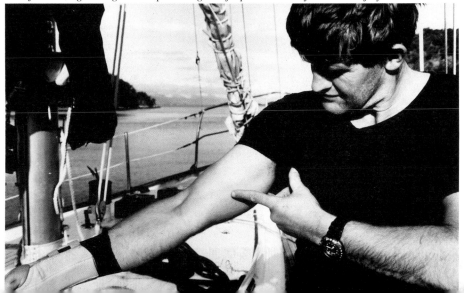

A dreaded williwaw: ashore just in the nick of time. At Puerto Williams a dozen miles along the Beagle Channel, the windspeed registers 120mph.

Paddling into Puerto Williams, the remote Chilean naval base on Navarino Island.

AU NOM DE
L AMICALE INTERNATIONALE
DES CAPITAINES AU LONG COURS
CAP HORNIERS
EN SOUVENIR DE TOUS
NOS PASSAGES DE CE CAP

JRN NOVEMBRE 1989

"We've done it Mum."
Typing a message for the satellite
to relay to the croft at Ardmore.

Boycie interviews a native for ITN.

First lady of Cape Horn. Out of the north-west swell it is calm at last, right under the 424-metre cliffs of the Cape.
The victorious team: standing left to right, Aled Williams, Nigel Tedeschi, Patto, Nigel Dennis, Lucho, Jack Tolson, Hoppy (Mark Hopking); seated left to right, Conrado Alvarez Diaz, JW (Jon Williams), Dad, Igor Asheshov, Bec, Chris Unsworth, Lieut. Eduardo Gahona, Boycie (John Boyce). (Richard Morris Adams is absent.)

weren't sorry to leave next day. The grassy hillside was terraced in thin winding grooves, made by years of sheep, mules and men walking in wet weather, to and from their small plots of land, called *chakras*. Don Pancho took one of the higher grooves, and we followed, though I was beginning to doubt if he knew the way, he seemed to rely on meeting people. Four hundred years ago, the Spaniards had quickened their pace here, hot on the heels of the last Inca, barely a couple of days from the stronghold of Vilcabamba, off to the north of our own route. I looked down at my rather tatty walking boots with their toes all scraped from years of walking the quartzite scree slopes of the Foinaven Ridge at home. Here in the Andes people looked enviously at them. Their own feet were usually cut, cracked and caked in mud, their motor-tyre sandals offering little protection. This was probably the first time such footprints had been left on this particular Inca road.

I was feeling pretty good, no stiffness from the rather long first day, and glad to see that there were plenty of clouds in the sky; it would not be too hot for a couple of hours yet. That morning, we walked through several lost valleys, remote out-of-time places. Igor showed us a primitive palm tree growing wild on the hillside, which was much sought after on the patios of Lima. His mother had asked him to collect cuttings for her garden, and I wondered if he was thinking of adding a nursery garden to his farm up in the hills outside Lima; maybe this would be more successful than the cider and honey ventures he'd already tried.

Lambras proved to be at the top of a hill and I felt the familiar altitude-related thumping in my head as we climbed up in the heat of the day, now the sun had burnt off the protective clouds. Antonio and his son-in-law were away from home, working on their chakra, and would not return before evening, so we were installed on the open porch of the thatched dry-stone sleeping hut, and his wife, Antonia, plied us with a large enamel plate of small potatoes boiled in their skins. We were starving, having eaten nothing since the mutton stew of the previous night. Boiled potatoes are the staple diet up on the altiplano, and the Peruvians are proud of giving the potato to the world.

Antonia kept herself to herself in her cooking hut but a small girl of nine or ten came rather timidly out with an empty bucket. Once past us, she ran off to the water spout to fill her pail, returning at full speed with the water splashing everywhere; I thought major cooking must be going on inside. She was a beautiful child, in a faded orange, yellow and green crocheted hat with a red rolled-up brim, pulled down to just above her fine eyebrows. Her face was round, her small flat nose barely stood proud from her face and most striking were her plump chapped cheeks. As the afternoon wore on, she became braver, sometimes standing at the doorway looking across the path at us; occasionally a smile would flash across her face for a second, before she dashed back inside to the safety of her grandmother.

The afternoon grew colder, thick mist rolled in, engulfing both buildings. It would be another cold night. Two men walked up the slope from behind the cook house and we introduced ourselves and handed over a letter from Raoul to the older of the two men. He was small and wiry with a big friendly smile. Raoul had told us Antonio loved going to Capiro, because it was always a bit of an adventure. I hoped he was feeling adventurous now, for without him our plan to reach Olaf would founder.

Antonio spoke no Spanish and he'd never learned to read, so our negotiations proceeded in a three-cornered way via Don Pancho and Igor, who explained our connections with the Bergs and how vital it was for us to get to Capiro and meet Olaf. Tilting his head on one side and smiling, Antonio went into the cook house. After a while I couldn't stand the suspense and went in too. It was also getting cold. The cook house was warm and dark except for the redness of the glowing fire. I sat down on a log close to the fire, my eyes smarting with the smoke, but gradually getting used to the dark. Sitting there, listening, but understanding very little, I felt extremely happy; it was all so real, no one was putting up a false front. These people were concerned with survival, not what clothes they were going to put on tomorrow, or where they were going on holiday. Everything was so simple and immediate.

Antonia squatted by the fire on her broad, cracked bare feet, making coffee. She passed me the first mug. Delicious, black and sweet. After a few laughs and stories, we came to the real business. Igor translated our ideas into the local Spanish for Don Pancho, who translated into Quechua for Antonio. All this took some time; bargaining is a very important part of life here. All the while, we watched Antonio's expression. The first vital question was: "Will Antonio guide us to Capiro?"

"Yes, he's keen to go, but he has much work to do here at Lambras. Antonio asks how long you want to stay at Capiro?"

"I should think a couple of days will be enough," Dad said, and the talk rolled on, back and forth. Antonio thought we would take another three and a half days to get to Capiro. This would make a total of five and a half days from Yupanca. Even at this distance the legend of Olaf was beginning to build: Antonio told us Olaf used to walk and run from Capiro to Yupanca in two days!

I went outside to get away from the smoke for a moment and think about the journey ahead. Dad had told us that when he'd been at Osambre in 1970, Olaf had been away on a hunting trip, only returning on the last day they were there. In those days he'd been young and strong, but quite shy and quiet compared with the other brothers. Now I imagined a rather outwardly gentle middle-aged man, with a wife and a couple of sons, rather as his father, Abel, had been. He'd have strong principles, and always be working. I imagined Capiro to be a guarded fort with Indians in the jungle all around, warding off danger and killing to protect their respected leader, Olaf. Don Pancho was always telling us how Olaf grew "*bustante*" (plenty) cocoa, we would have chocolate all the time. As a near chocoholic, this sounded great to me. I imagined us arriving at Capiro, exhausted – just as they'd arrived at Osambre in 1970. Olaf would take us in and feed and look after us. This was how it would be, I was sure.

"Supper's ready, Bec!" Igor called from the doorway, and I crept back into the cook house for a bowl of potato soup, with a little of our rice and a small leathery lump of gristly meat. The meat was in celebration of our visit. I'd seen it earlier, hanging on the wall and curing in the smoke. I had been hoping we wouldn't have to eat it, but now there was an empty space on the wall. After the soup, we ate savoury *tamales*, made from ground maize, egg, salt and water, mixed into a paste similar to mashed potato, then wrapped in the outer leaves of corn cobs and steamed. They were delicious. I remembered large women selling these on trains and buses in 1985; the smell was always very tempting, but we couldn't risk the stomach problems, so we'd never bought them.

Antonio was roasting more coffee beans in a small cast-iron pot, stirring them with a stick as they smoked. After eating, everyone was in high spirits at the prospect of the adventure ahead. Roberto and Simeon were particularly excited; very few people had ever been beyond Pampa-conas before, and tomorrow we would drop thousands of feet, down into the empty jungle. I'm sure they were dreaming of fighting the terrorists single-handed, and finding nuggets of gold in the jungle rivers. We were all looking forward to the bananas, tomatoes and chocolate Don Pancho had told us of.

It was almost dark as we laid out our sleeping-bags for the night. I couldn't decide whether to sleep outside on the open porch of the sleeping house, where it would be cold, or on the floor in the cook house with all the guinea-pigs. After some deliberation, I chickened out of the cook house idea, and went for the cold instead. I noticed the whole Huamani family slept together in one large bed, not removing any clothes, and just pulling a blanket over themselves. They would be warm anyway.

7

Into Sendero Country

"I'm cold," I said, wriggling around, trying to find a warm patch I might somehow have missed in my sleeping-bag. It was 4.30 a.m.

"Well, get up, you lump, you'll soon warm up."

Could this be my father? Of course it could.

Antonia came out of the sleeping-house and disappeared into the cook house to begin her chores. Roberto cooked us a large pan of rather runny rice pudding, giving us each two mugfuls in our mess tins. It was feeding time for the pigs too, and Antonia brought a large pan of potato peelings out of the cook house, which she tipped into a trough, crudely hollowed from a log. The large pigs grunted deeply with excitement, and the children pulled their ears. Antonia had a pained expression on her lined old face as she hit the greedier pigs with a stick and made wonderful cross hissing noises. This seemed a typical Quechua habit – the women have fierce tempers which snap at the slightest hint of trouble.

The small children came to life as the sunlight seeped over the hill-side, and ran to and fro, playing with two young collie puppies. The children had been given nothing so far, and now they sat cross-legged round the fire eyeing our black pot of rice pudding and keeping themselves warm. I'd had more than my fill, so I gave the rest of my breakfast to a young boy, waving my index finger round the circle to make clear that it must be shared, and they started eating rapidly.

We walked for four and a half hours, with one stop, up to the Usnuyoc pass at 13,000 feet. Antonio was going to catch up with us at his jungle farm at Monte Beron in a day and a half's time. He had things to sort out before leaving. There was not much chat among us, because we were all lost in our own thoughts. Anyone we met from now on was likely to be a Sendero, or at least a sympathiser. There were very few people around now, hardly any dwellings, and most of those were derelict. We saw two women with a baby, and they cowered away from the path when they saw us coming. Later on, there was a ragged man keeping an eye on three thin grazing mules. He looked at us and smiled. What was he doing here, where no one else lived? What did he know, that we didn't, with that strange smile? Don Pancho checked the route with him and we kept going.

We stopped for a break on the pass, Abra Usnuyoc, sucking hard on bitter-lemon Peruvian boiled sweets. It was eerie up there, with the mist slowly swirling around. To the left of the path lay a small graveyard. All Souls' Day had been only a few days before, and even in this desolate place, some of the graves had been tidied and new crosses added.

Once over the *abra*, the path soon turned steeply downwards and the vegetation began to change. I was astonished how quickly we entered the rainforest fringe, with plants similar to the climb up from Yupanca to Pampaconas. We were to descend all day long. On the map, Capiro looked to be close to the Apurimac, 10,000 feet lower at around 3,000 feet. Now Igor came last, his great enthusiasm for plants making him stop and exclaim, "This is amazing, wow," as he dived from side to side of the path. We were in a sea of vegetation, in varying shades from dark green to grey and creamy yellow. It was like visiting a botanical-garden glass house without the name tags. Igor pointed out *Bromelias Pinquin*, with spiny sword-shaped greenish-grey leaves, belonging to the pineapple family. It produces a red flower and grows high up in trees. Bamboo grew all over the place in great clumps, the stalks varying in thickness and height from a drinking straw to a large drainpipe. Rubber plants and yuccas, just like those in doctors' waiting-rooms back home, grew wherever they could find space and light, and this was usually next to the path. Trees of all ages stood silent, their leaves motionless, the thick branches and trunks of the giants festooned with wiry grey moss hanging down like old spiders' webs.

At home I enjoy the feeling of solitude, but here it was different: we were becoming increasingly worried about the presence of terrorists. Dad found a shotgun cartridge box on the path. It was eight or nine years since the Senderos had begun to terrorise this area, and their frightful night raids had long since made sure there were no people left down here in the jungle. All the old paths were overgrown now and I think it was the very stillness of plants and trees which frightened me most; I would turn quickly, imagining something or someone was watching me from behind one of them. If the Senderos did know we were here, which was fairly likely, we could quite easily meet them on this, the only path towards Capiro. I thought back to the Guardia Civil lieutenant in Pucyura who had told us he wouldn't come into this area with less than one hundred armed men at any time.

Don Pancho was getting impatient with us, he wanted to push on down to Antonio's chakra on the Torolyunca river. He had no interest at all in the plants; so we strode down the path, trying to keep up with him. On the steep mountainside the path had eroded into a deep gully, a sort of drain for the tropical rain. It would have been a good place for the Sendero to set an ambush. We'd been practising a drill to counter ambush, jumping off the path in different directions and circling back to a constantly up-dated rendezvous further back along the track. There didn't seem much chance of getting out of the deep green tunnel, but I couldn't think of a better idea.

When at last we came out into the hot bright sun again, we were in a sea of green and we stood silenced by the wonder of it all, while butterflies of every shape, size and colour fluttered around. Now I could understand how Dad had come up with his story of "Down the Amanoz" when I was a child. And now my ears were filled with all those jungle noises he used to perform for me, the crickets, grasshoppers and frogs, the strange brilliantly coloured birds screeching to each other. I just couldn't get enough of it all.

Far below, we could now see what we thought must be Toronc, Antonio's chakra; it was two small thatched jungle huts on the only flattish patch of ground for miles around, just where the long white beard of a tributary joined the Torolyunca river. Tiny patches of land had been cleared, and crops planted. Maybe other people lived here? I heard a baby crying, over and over again; I thought it might be coming from Toronc, but Igor said it was monkeys. When we arrived at the huts, there were no children, only Don Pancho, sitting on a log and gazing at the white ruins of his bare feet, bleached by the wellie boots.

Don Pancho pulled a handful of thatch from the roof of the bamboo-pole hut, and lit it with a match from the box he kept for his fags. Within a few seconds he had a fire going and hot sweet coffee soon perked us up. Then all we could think of was going for a swim in the river which roared along, ice cold and crystal clear, less than fifty yards

71

from the hut. Dad was already setting up his three-ounce carbon-fibre fly-rod, but even he wanted to swim before fishing. Roberto and Simeon arrived with the horses that carried our kit; we had one more day with the horses and then they were to be left behind as the going was too rough for them on the last bit of the journey to Capiro.

Many people get gold fever in this area. The dream of finding a nugget, several kilos in weight, in the Apurimac is hard to shake off. Bathing my hot and weary feet, I found myself looking into the water. It would be silly to stub my toe on a fortune and not notice. After lunch Dad's first job was to clean and zero the .22 rifle which Raoul had lent for our protection. It was fine-looking Remington repeater, but it hadn't been used or cleaned for some years. Dad removed the bolt, and decided it needed a good cleaning. Then came a rather fraught moment: trying to slide the bolt back in without oil wasn't easy, it didn't seem to fit into place properly. Don Pancho suddenly came awake – it was his son's gun, he was very proud of it. Luckily, after a bit of wiggling, the dry bolt slipped back into the breech and face was saved.

I fetched our tin of Ko-cho-line, a deep-red grease which we rubbed on our feet to keep the skin soft and supple. The tin said "no Sportsman, Private House or Stable should be without it". Its many uses were mostly to do with treating saddles and leather gear, but it also claimed to be the "Best Lubricant and Anti-Corrosive Dressing for Guns, Saddlery, Buckles, Golf Clubs, Garden and Farm Implements, Clipping Machines, Motors etc". Dad called importantly for a piece of rag to use as a pull-through, and I cut the pocket flap off a worn-out cotton shirt he'd handed on to me to wear at nights. The cleaning began . . . and went on for some time. Dad was in his element.

Igor told Don Pancho, Roberto and Simeon how Dad had served in the British Army, and "was truly a great fighter". After the Falklands War, when of course Peru supported Argentina, the Brits were looked upon as pretty tough; therefore, anyone who had served in their army must be quite something, particularly if he'd reached the rank of captain. Our three guides stood back, looking on with great excitement, even Don Pancho seemed impressed.

Tearing a side off one of the cardboard boxes which were supposed to be holding our supplies together, Dad drew a black cross in the middle, and a large black dot in the middle of that, then he powdered the cross with white chalk dust. I jammed it in among some stones at a gable end of the hut, so it was a couple of feet above the ground, and ran off to the side. It was my job to number the bullet holes, shouting where the bullet had pierced the target. Dad lay on his front in the long grass twenty-five yards away and took aim.

I heard the crack of the first bullet; it pierced the target about two inches high and a tiny bit left. The second, one and a quarter inches high and on the same line as the first. The third was half an inch down, and one inch to the left, but Dad didn't count this one, saying he'd pulled it. The group formed by the first two rounds showed us that the rifle shot slightly high and a tiny bit to the left. We couldn't afford any more ammunition, so if we all remembered it was firing a little high, we should be all right. It was hard to imagine what I would do if I actually found myself trying to remember all that while pointing it at a human being.

After that the afternoon turned into a fishing contest. Roberto was a desperately keen fisherman. But so was Dad. He taught me to cast a fly on to a dinner plate on the grass in front of the croft when I was very small, and I was given a fishing rod for my sixteenth birthday. I remember opening it in front of all my friends at boarding school, and being thrilled. So we all dug for worms, and all the men, except Don Pancho, set up their lines in the thundering icy water which was a trout-fishing legend. "*Truttas grande!*" people had cried when they heard we were coming here. "*Bustante truttas.*"

It was no contest. No sooner had Roberto with his handline thrown his little spinner, or *mariposa*, across the river than he pulled out his first fish; and his dark brown face split with a huge white grin of triumph. Jumping barefoot from one hot boulder to another, he and Simeon fished the tumbling pools at breakneck speed, and ended with a catch of twenty-two modest-sized trout.

Dad was determined to answer this by catching the big one, so he walked up the riverbed looking for likely pools. Raindrops began to fall like ping-pong balls. Should we give up and admit defeat (but not get totally soaked) – or should we keep on going, hoping to catch one big fish (but get drenched, with little chance of drying our clothes in the steaming jungle night)? Being Ridgways we had chosen the latter. We lost the hook and weight, and arrived back at the two huts half an hour later, completely drenched and without a fish. Roberto and Simeon were gutting their twenty-two, having returned just before it had begun to rain.

73

It wasn't a bad night, but the possibility of something crawling into my sleeping-bag if I unzipped anything made it a stuffy one.

"Meesta, Meesta, *buenos dias*." The door creaked open. Roberto always called Dad "Meesta" and Dad sometimes thought he detected a little sarcasm in it which put him into a slightly bad mood. But this could not last long with a breakfast of deep-fried crispy trout in prospect. Our guides ate theirs heads and all; I had never eaten a fish head before, and didn't really fancy the idea, but in these situations it is best not to upset the cook. It didn't taste too bad, just a bit bony and dry.

One of the horses was lame, so Roberto and Simeon stayed behind to redistribute the loads and Igor sorted out his plant collection while the rest of us set out behind Don Pancho who kept up such a pace that when a man appeared ahead out of the darkness of the trees, we all cannoned into one another like in a comedy film. He was dressed in vaguely military fatigues and cradled a huge axe and machete in an arm grooved with muscle. The stranger and Don Pancho spoke in rapid Quechua and I tried to get some clue from our guide's expression, but he always looked rather grim, so this was not very reassuring. After what seemed like ages, but was probably only a few seconds, the stranger's face broke into a wide grin. This was Antonio's son, taking part of the coffee crop out to market. The Huamanis were the only family still brave enough to come into the jungle in this area because they would not let their hard work go to waste at Toronc and Monte Beron which was our destination.

After a shy greeting to the three of us, Antonio's son strode on along the way we had come, followed shortly by four mules, laden with sacks of unroasted yellowy-green coffee beans. The first mule had a rifle tucked into its load strapping. A young woman brought up the rear of the procession, carrying a naked baby wrapped in a cloth, tied close to her back in a black manta.

An hour into the walk, it started to rain. This was the tropical rain-forest after all. The forest was getting taller and denser now, though the canopy still let through the heavy rain. I was constantly amazed at the size of everything, it was like looking through a permanent magnifying glass; leaves were enormous, snails were huge, and strange thorns on some of the trees were like sharp curved darning needles – I could see how Alice felt in Wonderland.

We followed the only narrow cleared route; when we came to a fork,

Don Pancho would stop and peer both ways before continuing. He had obviously not been this way for several years, and I dreaded the idea of being lost, or having to retrace our tracks. We followed the Torolyunca river downstream, losing height rapidly, until after six hours of solid walking – five in heavy rain – the path began to climb away from the river, its roar becoming fainter with every step. But now, to our left and right, there were coffee bushes; some of the beans had already ripened and fallen to the ground to be eaten by a host of small creatures. Climbing slowly up the valley side, we passed through more overgrown chakras of banana trees and maize. The path levelled out and then began to descend gently through more unkempt coffee, bananas and maize, past a strange contraption that looked like a giant clothes mangle but Don Pancho said was a sugar cane press, on until, through the undergrowth, we came to a long low building with a corrugated-tin roof, and a small thatched hut with mud walls into which Don Pancho disappeared, disgruntled at being so wet. We had reached Monte Beron.

We followed him in. A large bunch of small green bananas and two ripening papayas hung near a pile of grey ash where the fire had last been lit. High up on the back wall was a shelf, blackened by woodsmoke, holding a selection of maybe thirty skulls, mostly of different sorts of rodents, with long noses and huge front teeth; some were like small humans, but we hoped these would be monkeys.

Soon, much to our relief, Antonio appeared at a jog along the path we had come. He had probably set off from Lambras that morning. Seeing us looking at the skulls, he proudly pointed to one much larger one, telling us this had belonged to a black bear which he'd shot on the chakra; and he showed us the skin. All animal skins are saved here, but they don't bother to make them soft and supple, they are used as insulation from the ground, for sleeping on, and are unusually just stretched and dried in the sun.

The rain stopped, and soon the sun was burning away the misty clouds which had been shrouding the tree-covered ridges and valleys. Igor, Roberto, Simeon and the two horses arrived with tales of loads slipping. Everything seemed a lot better as the sun warmed us. The money Dad had been carrying in his pocket was laid out to dry on the sugar press, and Malc and Igor went off to discover what was growing here. They returned with some small oranges, but most of the fruit was still green. There were grapefruit, sweet lemon, orange, papaya, mango and banana trees as well as tomatoes, maize and all sorts of edible tubers. Monte Beron is at roughly the same altitude as Osambre and, as the crow flies, very close. In 1970 Dad had thought Osambre the Garden of Eden, and this was how I saw Monte Beron now. We washed our kit, hanging it in the trees to dry, and I washed my hair, a real luxury – having clean hair makes me feel a hundred per cent better.

Antonio rushed about with panfuls of roots making supper, while we looked out across many valleys, coming in from all directions, and worked out from our map that Osambre was just over the ridge opposite us. I thought how strange it must be for Dad to be so close to Osambre, and how sad he would feel that there were no longer Bergs there. Twenty years before, he'd written how he hoped there would be Ridgways at Ardmore as long as there were Bergs at Osambre. It was a sombre thought.

We discussed plans for going on down the river from Capiro, but this would depend upon what Olaf advised. With one horse now sick, and the chance of maybe the other two being eaten by jaguars when we left them here tomorrow, the prospect of having to carry all our own gear 12,000 feet back up on to the altiplano was not too cheering. I think Dad was looking for a bit of excitement too.

As it grew dark, we watched the huge deep-orange sun setting. Then, armed with our spoons and mess tins, crept into the cook house for supper: bowls of steaming yucca soup, with a plate of boiled sticks of white yucca in the centre of the table. There was also a small saucer of aptly named *ahi*, an exceptionally hot sauce made from green and red chillies. Knowing Dad is not keen on yucca, Antonio had made a special concoction for him of *oncochu*, a round grey root that tasted a lot nicer than the often woody yucca. There was plenty of food to go round, and seconds for everyone. Antonio was rolling with laughter at the way the gringos put too much ahi in their soup. Igor loved ahi, and he took much more of it than we could ever manage. Dad, never to be outdone, tried desperately to match Igor, breaking out in a sweat, with tears pouring down his puffed-out cheeks.

Feeling pleasantly full, we sat around the fire talking about the next few days and the journey to Capiro. The conversation was fairly slow because of the translating which had to be done with Antonio. Tomorrow we should reach Nueva Esperanza, which translated very suitably for us into New Hope. According to Don Pancho, there was a house there, but no people; but when we asked Antonio, he said there were some people there. Typically South American, Don Pancho often told us what he thought we wanted to hear, ignoring the real facts!

"Why can't the horses go on?" asked Malcolm. "Why leave them here, if the jaguars are going to eat them?"

Antonio replied that we would have to travel along a new route, which his son had cut only a week before, and this was far too steep, narrow and overgrown for horses to manage. This sounded exciting, trail-blazing *Boys' Own* stuff but, in reality, I was sure it would be hard work. Dad wondered what it was we were trying to avoid by taking a new route, but even Igor couldn't extract an answer for this.

We asked about the bountiful game in this emptied rainforest. Igor's tales of parrot soup were followed by Don Pancho's preference for the delicious taste of large black monkeys. Antonio offered us a monkey feast for the next day if we allowed him time to do some hunting. Monkey, he added casually, tasted just like a small person!

Antonio made space for us to lay our bedding on the coffee-bean drying racks in the big shed next door. I heard his quiet voice muttering, "Monte Beron, Monte Beron," contentedly from his own corner and then I was asleep.

The next day was expected to be our toughest yet, and we would now be carrying our own packs. Was it an omen that one of our horses had been bitten by a vampire bat in the night? A trickle of blood ran from its back right down one leg. We had read in the *Lima Times* about some miners on the Apurimac dying from rabies after being bitten by vampires. Roberto dabbed the horse's wound with some of the alcohol we used to light the Optimus and told us it would recover. A human might not have been so lucky.

We hadn't gone far when it became apparent the new route really was new. I could barely make it out and Antonio up ahead was still clearing it with his machete. A cry of "Jaguar!" rippled back along the line and Antonio pointed to fresh tracks on our path. This meant the horses, now left on their own at Monte Beron, could be in some danger. Antonio said they were in the hands of God. But they weren't his horses.

Our progress was slow, desperately steep and sweaty. Dad and Malc kept getting their rucksacks caught on vines and branches because the path had been cleared to the height of a Peruvian male, not for giant gringos. It was not too bad for me. But I was frightened many times that day by the landslides we crossed above vast drops. I knew that in theory you should not lean in to the hill when crossing a landslide because you only encouraged the slide, but it took more nerve than I had to lean out.

The plants too were hostile. Great barbed tendrils waved across the route, with giant stinging nettles whose sting matched the size of their leaves. Don Pancho taught us the difference between monkey and parrot calls, but I think he was just trying to keep our spirits up. In the late afternoon we came out on to a thin ridge and, as the sun was sinking, heard the sound of the Pampaconas river far below. The descent in the dark was frightening and painful. We became separated, and I cried, as quietly as I could in the darkness, in sheer desperation.

As the sound of the river grew deafening we found ourselves beside its bank and there was Antonio setting up camp. Small insects fluttered everywhere around us. Roberto shone the torch on them and I could see they were silvery moths, thousands of them, attracted maybe by the salt in our sweat. Just to our left was a huge boulder and from the top of it a wooden bridge, built by Antonio's son only a few days before, led across the river. I marvelled how Antonio had brought us all to this exact spot in the dark, as I fell into exhausted itching sleep.

8

Jaguar

Antonio sat casually on the wooden bridge, one leg hanging down through the gap, the other bent up under him. His son had spanned the river, but it was too wide to cross with just one trunk, so two-thirds of the way over, the top of the first tree was lashed to a shorter trunk which reached the far side. The bridge itself was very narrow, hardly two feet wide, and Antonio was busily lashing thin branches together with bark to form a sort of horizontal ladder. It looked quite tricky to me, and I hoped he'd fix more pieces in place before I had to cross. The morning light had shown us for the first time just how high above the thundering torrent the whole contraption was.

We packed our kit quickly, drinking hot and watery rice pudding. Our guides looked anxious this morning, a new bridge was an obvious target. They were constantly on the look-out, and our camp fire could have been a beacon during the night. Igor passed the message to Dad that Roberto, who carried the rifle, would like to have some ammunition for the walk today, just in case. Dad agreed to give him ten rounds, with one in the breech. This really excited Dad, and he gave us instructions about what to do if we were attacked, which largely amounted to looking mean, tough and angry, and telling them we were bloody well British and would not stand for any of this nonsense. I imagined an attack would be more along the lines of a Vietnam film: blackened faces, burning and shooting, with no time for us to explain why we had come.

With breakfast over, our guides were itching to get going. The time had come to cross the bridge. Thankfully, Simeon had taken my rucksack. Like moving along the deck of the yacht in rough weather, I tried to keep three points of contact at all times. Half way across, and the bridge was at its maximum bendiness, swinging gently as I moved my weight. The roll of Karrimats I was carrying had now flopped round in

79

front of me, slightly hampering my vision, but I knew I had to continue, with the frantic sound of the rushing water below me blocking out all shouts of encouragement from the bank. I was alone. My arms and legs were beginning to ache with the tension. I crawled on and reached the other side with enormous relief.

At first, the going was much better than the previous day. As we passed through abandoned chakras where the bananas and coffee were growing wild, Roberto cut down a large bunch of bananas and hid them under some leaves so they'd be ready on the way back. The heat was intense, we were soon drenched in sweat. My hair was tied back, but kept getting caught in the branches. I wondered about the wisdom of having long hair in these situations, but local women had longer hair than mine. We pressed on. After a couple of hours, and not much rest, we were back up on to flatter land. The vegetation was not so dense now, and I was amazed at Roberto's skill in following the trail Antonio and Don Pancho had made. Only overturned leaves on the ground and the odd snapped twig showed the way.

"Jaguar! Jaguar!" Roberto shouted with excitement, pointing at a paw print in the dirt.

"Oh yeah!" I said wearily to Dad. "Trying to liven up the old gringos I should think, showing us the sights."

Igor knelt down showing Dad the clear print of the paw. "Roberto says it's following Pancho."

There was a chuckle from Roberto and Simeon, which confirmed my suspicion that this print could be days old. We came up on to a steep ridge with a narrow path along it and scrubby trees falling away on both sides; I was wary, feeling rather insecure on such a narrow path. If there really was a jaguar following Don Pancho, it could not be far ahead.

In the distance there was a faint cry, which quickly rippled back through the line, gaining in volume and excitement.

"Jaguar!" Roberto and Simeon both shouted.

My first reaction was to reach for my camera and rush forward, urged on by Dad, finger poised over the red button. We were now at the end of the spur, huddled together on a small mossy mound. Way below was a narrow torrent of white water, bridged by a couple of stout trees, but no sign of the jaguar. "I've missed it," I thought. But Don Pancho was still going crazy, jumping up and down, on the opposite bank, only ten feet across the deep chasm. He kept pointing just below where we were standing, and we began to realise there were two jaguars in a cave only a few feet below us.

Once we had all joined him across the water, Don Pancho told Igor, in a hoarse rapid voice, what had happened. He and Antonio came to the bridge, Antonio crossed and, as Pancho followed, a large jaguar appeared at the mouth of the cave, only a few feet from the bridge, snarling and waving its giant paws at Pancho, who nearly fell off the bridge with fright. Antonio, who carried his own shotgun, fired at the beast, hitting it and forcing it back into the cave, wounded. This was quite a shock for old Don Pancho, who was used to a quiet life in Lucma, getting his own way, his days of youthful bravery and jungle hunting long gone.

If there really was a wounded beast in the cave, we ought to put it out of its agony. We were also desperate to see this king of the Amazon jungle. Antonio cut a couple of long thin jungle saplings to goad the jaguars to the front of their cave, as Roberto lay still with the shotgun and Dad with the rifle, trained on the mouth of the cave. Butterflies landing on the gun barrels had to be brushed aside to line up the sights.

Antonio walked back along the tree-trunk bridge a little way, and poked one of the long sticks into the cave; nothing happened for a moment, then the stick shook violently, as if something with immense strength had got hold of the other end. Antonio struggled to keep his footing on the bridge, then pulled the pole backwards. The end had been chewed as if it were a pencil. He thrust the pole into the cave again, and suddenly a huge jaguar came forward out of the darkness. Its eyes shone green in the light like emeralds, and its beautiful striped head moved quickly from side to side as its powerful jaws chewed the end of the stick. Don Pancho began to shout, Antonio dropped the pole, Dad squeezed the trigger, but the gun did not fire. He ejected the dud bullet and took aim again, but the jaguar was gone.

The dropped pole was now wedged some ten feet down the chasm wall, and so there was a pause in the action while Simeon got it back and the goading began again. The jaguar soon came to the front of the cave, its movements liquid, lifting a huge paw to swipe at the aggravating pole, before grabbing it again in its powerful jaws. Now its whole head was visible from the narrow cave mouth, ears pinned back, snarling with anger, its mouth opening to show long white fangs. Don Pancho was shouting, "Aye, Aye, Aye!" One shot rang out, and another. Then the beast fell motionless to the cold stone. The shots sent a shiver down my spine. The excitement was gone, the beast dead.

Don Pancho was sure there was still another in the cave, and kept shouting, "*Un autra mas! Autra mas!*" Dad said he felt a bit shaken. He didn't like shooting animals, apart from the odd hoodie crow at lambing time. But this was the jungle. However, he kept aim, with four more bullets in the magazine, while Roberto bravely climbed down to the cave, gingerly looked in, and on seeing nothing in the darkness, pulled the dead beast out with the help of Antonio. They held it by its four paws, and its limp body hung helplessly between them. It was male; its mate, thankfully, must have escaped during the frenzy. Only now could we see its real size.

Our four guides were dying to have their photograph taken alongside the most feared animal in South America. The jaguar has been respected here for over three thousand years, for its power, hunting prowess and associations with death and fertility. Jaguar teeth and claws are still worn as ornaments at festivals, originally in the belief that the wearer will gain the animal's attributes. A tribe successful in battle used to be called jaguars, after the most successful predator in South America, except for man. Even now, the Quechua people believe in a flying feline god, called Ccoa, who roars like thunder, lightning coming from its eyes, and who spits hail and urinates rain.

Roberto and Simeon had never seen a jaguar before, so to witness the killing of this feared beast was a great occasion for them. To the four of us gringos the sight of that jaguar dead was unbearably sad. I bent to touch the limp body lying at my feet; it was warm, its fur short, smooth and soft, and it smelt perfectly clean. It reminded me of Jinja, one of our cats at home. She is sleek and smooth like this huge cat, and she hunts in the wood just as this beast had hunted in the jungle.

The jaguar's belly was a creamy apricot, darkening gradually to gold up its sides and along its back. Its spots were big and black on its underside, small and nearly round on its huge paws, each the size of a man's outstretched hand, with black scarred pads and four deadly claws. The spots linked together up the length of its legs, changing to a pansy shape on its sides with darker gold in the middle and often a black dot. The black shapes merged together along its backbone to form an almost continuous black line down its long black-tipped tail. Large black jungle eyes, ever-awake, mimicked its real eyes, which were now only half open and glazed in death. The inside of its mouth was as black as its spots, with a long pinky tongue, large grinding teeth and two pairs of perfectly interlocked fangs.

Still unsure what the killing of this animal really meant to our guides, particularly Antonio, I watched to see what would happen next. First, Antonio cut the black tip off the jaguar's tail and brushed it under his chin, grinning with joy. Then he skinned the beast, eagerly helped by Roberto and Simeon; Don Pancho stood by, giving advice and looking rather tired after all the excitement. Rolling up the skin, Antonio then gutted and butchered the carcass, calling us over to see a familiar bundle of black bristles and bones which filled the stomach. The jaguar must have been still digesting the pig when Don Pancho's scent entered its nostrils.

Nothing was to be wasted. Apart from the pig in the digestive tract, the only part which could not be saved was the blood, and I felt that was only because we didn't have a spare empty container. Everything was bundled up, making the heavy loads even heavier, but spirits were high, there would be plenty of *rico* meat for supper.

The rest of the day could not possibly live up to its start and when we eventually reached Nueva Esperanza it sorely belied its name. Some square patches of dried banana leaves had once been the roofs of houses, but with the inhabitants gone, they'd soon collapsed. Antonio went off to look for the one remaining family, who were probably watching us from the trees, waiting to see if we were to be trusted. He swapped a small amount of jaguar meat for the use of a pot and some food; but he warned us that any other dealings would have to be paid for with bullets. This was the only currency in these parts.

Dad and Igor tried to puzzle out the reasons for the rifle's misfire, and it turned out that, while Roberto was carrying the weapon, Antonio had put one of his own ancient bullets in the breech; this was the dud. Apparently the rule of the jungle has it that any animal killed belongs to the person whose bullet kills it.

Antonio arranged the salted meat on racks of horizontal poles which he built between trees, then he lit small fires underneath, which he fed with green wood to make plenty of smoke to cure the meat. The head and pieces of fat hung in a tree, next to joints waiting to be salted. The red meat was hardly visible through the black mass of flies, seething over its surface, and I imagined how Gran would retch at this sight!

The friends who'd lent Antonio the cooking pot arrived to see the strange gringos. A proud but painfully thin man, with the grey sweating face of malaria, Justo Argumendo looked as if he'd spent his life deprived of sunlight by the jungle canopy. He was followed everywhere by his sickly three-year-old son, Merlin. Nevertheless, he brought with him a blackened kettle full of hot sweet coffee, a bowl of cooked yucca and bowl of small bananas steamed in their skins. Eight years earlier, he and his young wife had moved into the jungle ahead of the terrorists, who'd raided his village high in the sierra on the other side of the Apurimac. They had worked hard, clearing small patches to grow their crops of cocoa and bananas. They depended on Olaf to help them get their cocoa to market and find a good price for it; and when times were hard, Justo panned for gold at Capiro.

Shortly after their arrival in Nueva Esperanza, the Sendero Luminoso had also come down from the sierra and begun moving into the jungle, seeing the dense canopy as a safe haven from prying helicopter patrols. Justo told us that at first the military supported the people of the jungle, issuing them with weapons and ammunition to protect themselves; but when Alan Garcia came to power in Lima, the military were told to demand the weapons back, and when the Sendero over-ran the area, the authorities stopped spraying against malaria. The inhabitants of Nueva Esperanza were the Forgotten People, he told us. Abandoned by those very authorities whom they had freely elected to government, most had left the jungle through fear, and fled to shanty towns on the outskirts of the cities, in search of non-existent work. As for Justo, his wife was too sick with malaria to complete the strenuous journey out to the nearest road.

Señor Argumendo spoke highly of Olaf, saying that he was expecting us, and worried for our safety. He told us about Olaf's gold-panning near Capiro. The murder of Elvin and the bloody battle which took place that day at Osambre was a well-known tragedy for miles around.

Soon after Señor Argumendo left, three other men who also knew Antonio arrived: they seemed to be the only other inhabitants of Nueva Esperanza. They talked to us about their plight, and asked us for ammunition. Antonio gave them a piece of jaguar meat, and one called Romulo agreed to return the next morning to help carry our kit on to Capiro.

Jaguar stew which had been simmering for some hours was served up in huge portions, and we sat around the fire dipping our yucca into the rich gravy. The meat was delicious, tasting quite gamey. But I could only think back to those green eyes at the cave entrance. What a magical beast the jaguar was.

The night was long and I woke up many times from my light sleep, due to some worrying dream or the heat. At one point there was pandemonium, as Roberto and Simeon leapt up shouting, "*Mono, mono, mono.*" They had been dying to catch a monkey ever since we had entered monkey country, and had praised monkey stew as "rico". By now I realised that any sort of meat or fish was "rico" compared to the normal stodgy diet of rice and yucca. There was a great deal of commotion as they chased off with the horse torch into the surrounding jungle, but the monkey was far too quick for them.

It was not very surprising to find jaguar stew was the only item on the breakfast menu. It would be sustaining. Romulo arrived to carry one of the rucksacks, his prize possession, an old rifle, slung over one shoulder and a small brightly coloured woven bag with tassels carried across his chest to hold the ammunition. He and Don Pancho were to go ahead, to warn the people of Capiro we were not far behind and make sure we weren't attacked.

Señor Argumendo arrived with his family to show the rest of the children their first gringos. Their skin was pale and clammy. The señora was quite different from the usual tough Quechua women. She looked at us shyly and smiled nervously, sweat already breaking out on her forehead. She was ill with both malaria and the worry of the encroaching Senderos. There would be little hope for her when they attacked. Her thin frame just managed to support a chubby baby on her back, and in front of her stood a bemused young girl with unkempt hair. She looked sternly up at us, amazed by our fair hair and height. I smiled at her, but she gave nothing away. I looked down at her bitten legs, and remembered the scars on Elizabeth's legs when she first arrived at Ardmore. I noticed the small girl had no toes, most likely the result of using pesticides and being unable to read the warning about protective clothing on the container.

Señor Argumendo asked us shyly and hopefully, when we would return. How difficult it was to say that we might never return. As we walked away from them, they stood ghostlike on the path, watching us. For a long time I could not get that innocent and helpless family, at the mercy of who knew what acts of terrorism, out of my mind. But now all our thoughts were concentrated on Capiro and our dreams of meeting with Olaf.

By the middle of the day we came to a saddle on a ridge; from here the path led downhill towards a vein of coffee-coloured water, banded here and there with skeins of white rapids. The river was the only colour change in the wide green space. We knew this was the Apurimac, the Great Speaker, into which many smaller tributaries flowed, itself a tributary of the Amazon. Capiro must not be far away, and all downhill. I imagined that by now, Olaf would be waiting for us, knowing our exact whereabouts from messages sent forward by trusty Indians who watched us invisibly from the trees. He would take us to his house, where there would be all sorts of fresh jungle foods laid out for us. His wife would make sure we were comfortable and encourage us to eat and drink. Olaf would listen to Dad telling him, in his broken Spanish, the profound effect Olaf's father Abel's philosophy of life and Osambre had had on him; and stories of the trip downriver with Elvin would be recounted. They would talk of "the good old days" and how it was then in the Garden of Eden.

We were walking all together now, realising it would be safer. Roberto pointed out foliage-covered pits that had been dug along the side of the path to trap anyone coming to attack Capiro by night. We passed a large freshly burnt area of jungle. Olaf must be clearing the ground to expand the cocoa production.

Romulo came back along the path to meet us. We followed in a line behind him, anxious at what was to come. The burnt ground smelt sweet, but the heat was intense. Suddenly we came to a T-junction on the path and stopped. To our right was a bamboo shack, and there sat Don Pancho, eating a fried egg off an enamel plate. A young woman hovered behind him, looking nearly as sick as Señora Argumendo had done; she didn't acknowledge our presence, but maybe she was just shy. The path ran on down a slope and out of sight and a branch led off to some houses on stilts, from which young faces peered through the loose bamboo walls. A very thin and small man appeared, greeted our guides with a handshake and spoke a few words to them in a high-pitched squeaky voice, then ran off along the way we had come.

"Is this Capiro?" asked Dad. Romulo said it was. "Is Olaf here?" Dad asked hesitantly.

Romulo explained he was gold-panning some way upriver, but the man who had just run off along the path was a Campa Indian and he was going to tell him we had arrived.

This was all a bit of an anticlimax. We sat down in the shade and waited a couple of hours, sucking the white juicy pith inside cocoa-bean pods and enjoying a bowl of tomatoes with slices of avocado which a smiling man brought us. Still no Olaf.

We went down to the river and had a swim. The excitement of arriving at Capiro dwindled away, and I was beginning to realise that maybe this was not the Garden of Eden that Osambre had been nineteen years previously. The women and children sat around doing only the bare minimum. This was not a thriving community and they looked weary and resigned to taking whatever was to come. I tried to sleep with my head on my rucksack, but realised I was in for a bout of Montezuma's Revenge. As I was making a dash for it, somebody said, "Olaf's here."

9

Olaf

"Olaf is here!"

It was almost dark, I felt like death. Too many bananas and too much cocoa-bean pith mixed with dehydration had got me. Malc was also suffering, from the twenty-six bananas he had consumed earlier in the day. The four of us had been disheartened by the long wait. Why had Olaf not come to meet us? It was a ragged team that walked slowly up the path towards the junction where we had waited earlier in the day. There in the darkness we could just make out a group of maybe half a dozen men, each defined by the red glow of his cigarette. No one said a word. My head was spinning, my stomach turning and my legs felt weak, I was finding it hard to stand up. Even this big moment could not quite erase how ill I was feeling.

Luckily Dad was okay. He stepped forward, hand outstretched in the best of British manners. "John Ridgway," he introduced himself to a figure who stood apart, upright, with arms crossed and rifle slung across his back.

This was Olaf.

"Olaf Berg?" Dad said.

"*Si*," came the terse reply. There was tension in the air. Then Olaf continued, "I was expecting you. How long did it take you?" The words came out like gunfire.

"Seven days," Dad started to explain but was quickly interrupted.

"On my own, I do it uphill to Lucma in two and a half!" There was no compassion in this man. His supporters chuckled as if on cue.

"We've come to find out what really happened to Elvin."

Again Dad was cut short. I knew he would not take kindly to this, as Olaf embarked in his rifle-fire voice on the terrible story we had come so far, but seemingly not fast enough, to hear.

"We heard the terrorists were going to Osambre. Virgil and I went quickly from here to the farm to get Elvin. He wanted to have his guinea-pig breakfast and was in no hurry to leave. He kept on saying that they were his friends, they were not going to kill him. Around midday, just as we were about to leave, thirty-five terrorists arrived. A 'friend' from Lucmahuayco called Elvin out of the house. This was a trick. They seized him, tied him to a chair, poured kerosene on his beard and set it alight. They then burnt his arms, chest and legs. They stabbed him from front and back, crushed his skull with rocks – he was totally deformed." Olaf had been acting out this horrific description with his arms. There was silence all around. "They held me, forcing me to watch what they had done to my brother, then one of them put his rifle to my chest. Looking into my eyes, he pulled the trigger, but the rifle did not fire. I shot and killed two and escaped." He went quiet.

"What happened to Virgil?" Dad ventured, remembering the younger, fatter brother from 1970.

"During the attack, he was shot in the knee. One of the terrorists was sent in to see what state he was in. 'He's bleeding,' the man said. 'Well, make him bleed a bit more,' they said. Virgil shot him through the head as he came through the door. He fought on alone all day. At nightfall they threw in a stick of dynamite and left him for dead. He crawled into the jungle and lay there for two weeks, unable to move, until I found him. He was very weak, I brought him back here, he stayed in the house you're staying in. After a couple of months, he went mad and died, it was a drawn-out death, some kind of cerebral stroke."

Olaf became quiet again, not quite as aggressive as he had begun. Now he was the only Berg left – determined to avenge his brothers' murders.

How pathetic I was, being sorry for myself and feeling sick. We do not know real hardship. I was glad that the Berg parents, Abel and Delores, had died of natural causes a few years earlier, and did not have to witness this terrible end to Osambre, their dream. In 1985, we had asked everyone why the Senderos had wanted to murder Elvin like this, but there did not seem to be any known reason. Now Dad asked Olaf the same question.

"We always welcomed visitors, but ever since the 1965 revolution, there was a lot of hatred against our family. The police came in '65, they put a garrison in Osambre and dealt with the locals in a harsh way. We were always a target after that."

After a moment of quiet, and as if Olaf felt he was showing too much emotion, he was self-assertive again. He said he had often "willed" us to come, and now here we were. This showed the power of the mind. At this we felt welcomed, when only a few moments before he had seemed so hostile. Maybe we had passed some sort of a test.

"Do you know who killed Elvin?" Dad asked.

Olaf spat out the names, "Orrosco and Dias from Lucmahuayco", as if they were venom. "They have disappeared from this area. They are afraid of me."

Olaf began to explain that the Senderos had shot at him across the river that day, while he was gold-panning. This happened quite regularly. I thought of the few figures I had seen on the far bank while we had been bathing earlier. Olaf and his small team of warriors would respond by jumping aboard their rafts, paddling across the river and chasing the terrorists off.

It was dark now. "Come and have some food." Olaf was suddenly the host I had wanted to see him as.

We all followed him back down the path to Virgil's hut. Some women appeared with black cooking pots and Olaf dished out the beans and rice, telling us the Senderos had stolen all their cattle and pigs, so there was no longer any meat. Unfortunately, I still felt so ill I could hardly face the beans, which would have been a great treat.

Olaf's "warriors" ate too, the women disappeared without a word, and the Campa Indian, whom we had seen when we first arrived had now joined the circle. Olaf explained that he was Julio. He and Elvin had grown up together, and it was he who had buried Elvin. As Dad had thought, the photograph of Elvin he put in his book *Amazon Journey* was of Elvin with this man, backed by the emerald jungle. Now Julio looked worn, his quick smile had faded with the troubles, and he was as keen to avenge Elvin's death as Olaf. The Campas are a short, slightly built people who live deep in the jungle, known for their immense strength and fierceness. There was no conversation from Julio. Indeed there was little chat from any of the warriors. Meal times were for eating not talking. But Igor persevered and asked how they made a living; a little cocoa, a little gold, came the answer. This got Olaf on to his other favourite subject: gold. He asked if we knew of a special underwater metal detector that he could use in the river. There must be large nuggets trapped in cracks on the bed of the river, there might even be a huge seam – this was a man with gold fever.

Olaf began to explain to us that the people we saw here at Capiro were actually from Chiteni, a village further up stream on the other bank. "It was destroyed by the Senderos five months ago. Tomorrow we will visit Chiteni, and you can tell the authorities what happened there."

Once again Olaf was fired up with the passion of revenge. "If they catch me I'd better be dead. I need a cyanide pill. They will cut off my ears, puncture my eyes, cut off my genitals and stuff them in my mouth; disembowel me while cutting me to pieces. Young bestial children are trained to do it."

He remembered our presence. "You must leave Capiro quickly, there are Senderos all around. It is not safe for you to be here. You can't go downriver, it's too dangerous. Maybe we could blast a way upriver, through Osambre and Lucmahuayco . . ."

Olaf sounded excited at this idea, but I could just imagine us caught up in a gun battle. We wanted to accomplish the second part of our journey intact. Bringing Elizabeth's mother news of her daughter involved getting to Accobamba, and to do this we needed to go upriver or in a large circle through Ayacucho, back to Cuzco and along the usual route.

I knew Dad was set on going downriver, partly because his knee was very painful for battling up through the jungle, but also because he was keen to revisit some of the places he had been in 1970 with Elvin, and the smell of adventure ahead in the turbulent rapids of the Apurimac pulled hard at him. With Dad, the worse things sounded, the more he wanted to go and try his luck, so Olaf's warnings about the river fell on deaf ears. But Olaf had not finished.

"Below Lechemayo, you're into Narco country. Vast amounts of coca are grown there and turned into coca paste. There are small airfields hidden in the jungle close to the river. Colombian planes touch down for a few minutes to load up and off. This part of the river you would have to travel by dug-out canoe; if you are stopped, they cut your throat."

I knew this was no wind-up. The Narcos found the Senderos useful allies; offering the terrorists thirty thousand dollars for a dead American. The latest victim was a young journalist, kidnapped while investigating the coca farms and drug-trafficking for the *Tampa Tribune*, and found strangled with his hands tied behind his back. A placard next to him read, "This is how North American spies linked to the Pentagon die . . . Death to North American imperialism . . . Viva President Gonzalo . . . Death to George Bush." The words echoed the Sendero newspaper, *El Diario*.

If we reached San Francisco, we still had to travel a hundred and fifty miles to Ayacucho, the birthplace of the Senderos.

"There have been more deaths on that road than anywhere since the war began," Olaf continued. "Now we must sleep. I have no home, I sleep in the forest, somewhere different every night. They will never know where I am. They usually come between three and four in the morning. Goodnight."

He was gone into the darkness and his "warriors" drifted off in different directions. We stumbled into Virgil's house and Dad and I laid our bivvy bags and liners out on Virgil's death bed. How ragged the four of us were now. If attacked tonight what hope would we have?

"He's paranoid," I said to the others, "but if anyone has the right to be paranoid, it's him!"

Olaf arrived early next morning, bringing pork, chicken, yucca, steamed bananas and coffee for breakfast. We felt terrible to be eating their food, and the chickens were minute. Olaf's programme for us today was a foray across the river into Sendero country to witness the devastation of Chiteni so that we could report this to the authorities downriver. Eleven of us set off at a cracking pace along the edge of a burnt banana plantation, led by Olaf, barefoot, with a smart Czech rifle slung across his back. After an hour we came out on to the muddy riverbank, the roar of the torrent overpowering everything. Here the party fragmented and our four guides remained behind to try their hand at gold-panning. Further upstream we came across some hopeless-looking Indians intent on the same thing. One man rushed forward with six small lumps of gold wrapped in a crumpled banknote. I could not help noticing how smashed his thumb ends and nails were. One of the panners showed me how to use the pan properly, crouched in the shallows, swirling the gritty water round and round, spilling a little out at a time. But it was not going to be my lucky day.

Olaf explained how this Capiro gold rush had originated with an American called Johnson who came here in the thirties and sent nuggets by the kilo back to the USA. He died and was buried in the area in 1950 and folk have been searching, unsuccessfully, for his source ever since. Olaf is one of them, but seeing that he wasn't going to convert us to gold prospectors, as if to change the subject he untied a green and white cloth around his waist and tossed something that looked like an avocado to Dad.

"This'll take some peeling," Dad remarked, as he held up a hand grenade between finger and thumb. We laughed, suddenly very alive.

We were now set to cross the river. Olaf had three balsa-wood rafts ready, each about fifteen feet long and made from a half-dozen slim poles lashed together with bark. Igor had been worried about the advisability of my going any farther. But I was more concerned about being left behind. Apart from not wanting to get separated, I realised I didn't want to miss out on any of the excitement on the other side. Olaf clearly considered women as second class, never addressing any remark directly to la señorita, but he now assumed the responsibility of ferrying me over, and I knelt on the middle of the raft, adjusting my weight as bidden, while he stood at the back, his feet spread, and paddled upstream, working the eddy close under the cliff. The others followed, Dad scanning the jungle on the far bank for action. We were across the hundred yards of river in a few minutes and quickly into the trees, following an overgrown path through bananas and cocoa. Once Olaf waved us down into hiding, but it was only doves we had disturbed in the trees.

Chiteni was a ghost village built round a large grass square. Blackened walls were evidence that some of the houses had been burnt, others had been deserted suddenly, leaving domestic objects lying around intact. All the corrugated-iron roofs had been taken for use by the terrorists. As we sucked sweet lemons, pineapples and oranges, Olaf told the village's sorry story.

"Two years ago, the Senderos attacked the village. The Ronda was strong and drove them away. The Senderos dropped a gun as they fled, which the Ronda found and kept as their own. The army heard that the Ronda had captured this weapon, which had belonged to them, and came to the village as friends to collect it. But they got all the men together, tied them up, beat them and questioned them. Some of the soldiers drank heavily and raped many of the women. Eventually they found the weapon and left after stealing all the panned gold."

Olaf went on to explain that that was not the end of the story: the Senderos came back, the Ronda could no longer protect the village; some of the houses were burnt and about ten villagers killed. The rest fled, some to Capiro, others downriver. Their fifteen hundred hectares of cocoa now just rots.

This seemed a typically tragic South American muddle, where innocent weak people suffer at the hands of strong bullies. Surely something had to be done to help the people protect themselves. Earlier on they had been issued with weapons, but when the government changed, everything had to be handed back. This was how Olaf had the hand grenades.

Before we left, he pointed to a cleared grassy spur, back across the river and upstream a little. "That is where the herd of Charolais cattle from Osambre used to graze." His voice had the sad yearning, almost a longing to be back in those happy days of his youth. Dad could remember the fine large cows, and the pride with which Abel talked about them.

The trip back to the other bank was epic. I think Olaf was a little worried about shooting the worst rapids with me as his passenger, and we stopped on a sand bank in the middle of the river for him to discuss tactics with his two fellow *balseros*. But Olaf looked to be enjoying himself. A quick grin showed off his square front teeth outlined with gold, while his hitherto sober companions laughed with excitement, as we whizzed past the waving gold-panners, and came to a stop where we had left Don Pancho and our other three friends, who had already returned to Capiro, leaving behind them a moderate-sized crater in the bank.

After supper Olaf sat with us for some hours talking. Quick and intelligent, he had not seen anyone from outside for a long time and took this opportunity to talk over wider matters than most jungle folk have views upon. Inevitably we turned to politics. Perhaps, he said bitterly, the Senderos should become the government, then the people could become the terrorists! He denounced democracy for Peru, suggesting a dictatorship similar to that of Pinochet which had been so brutal for years in neighbouring Chile. He concluded from his understanding of the Bible that the anti-Christ was nigh. The conversation then got back to the gold, and a device Olaf said he had read of in *Popular Mechanics* which claimed to extract oxygen from the water. Perhaps Igor could find a way to get hold of this device, as well as the gold-detector, and bring them both to Capiro! Igor did not hold out much hope for such a project, so tried to change the subject. But Olaf continued to explain that he only wanted to find enough gold to enable him to go to Lima, buy a farm outside the capital where he could live out his days, and change his name for his safety. The Berg name would be extinguished from South America. Somehow, I could not see him as an old man sitting in a rocking-chair on a rickety veranda keeping an eye on his crops.

It was decided, after the rafting excitement of the afternoon, that Olaf would take us downriver. We should be ready early, and would need to get all our kit waterproofed for the treacherous journey ahead.

10

River Running

My knowledge of rafting came from those exciting photographs of people togged up in buoyancy aids and crash helmets grimacing with determination as they bomb through great masses of turbulent boiling water in sturdy-looking inflatable rubber rafts. I would like to try it one day, I thought, and now I was having my chance. Our rafting was not quite like the pictures. We were setting off on a trip which Olaf thought would take a day, but did not sound all that sure about, as no one ever travelled this journey. The river was officially unnavigable.

We said fond farewells to our four guides – Don Pancho, Antonio, Roberto and Simeon – who were setting off to walk back the way we had come, proudly bearing jaguar meat and great tales of how they had acquired it. We gringos would be remembered mostly for our fascination with washing our bodies and clothes, which our guides found really quite odd. They only bothered at the end of a journey, not twice a day.

Now was the moment of truth for Igor. Having said, "I've done a bit of rafting," he was to be alone. I was to go with Olaf again, Malcolm with Romulo and Dad with the best of the other balseros, who was called Saturnino.

Sooner than expected the first rapid appeared. It did not look too bad to me, but we were sucked towards it at great speed and I could see Dad and Saturnino bouncing through it ahead. Olaf paddled furiously to try and steer us, but to no avail. I hung on with white knuckles as great waves of warm muddy water broke over us. My first thought was to wish I had a waterproof camera, my second to realise that we were not in control, and suddenly I was underwater. This was not just a wave, I was under the raft, with my eyes open. I pulled my way to the edge of it before surfacing. Olaf was already up, his green cap still firmly wedged on his head. He looked quite relieved to see me, and signalled me to

96

climb on to the upturned raft, which I did quickly, just before being crushed between raft and rock face as we were sucked past smooth black walls.

I felt really quite exhilarated by this start to the day. In one way it had got rid of the nerves, but in another it had reinforced them. The rapid we had just come to grief in looked fairly average to me, surely there was a lot worse to come? Olaf paddled into an area of slack water close to the shore where Dad and Saturnino were recovering. They too had capsized. Dad was grinning with excitement.

"What would Gran say?" he greeted me.

My camera had suffered badly. Its automatic rewind had cleverly begun as soon as the riverwater penetrated it, saving the film, but for a few watermarks. But it emitted a sort of death scream until the battery died.

Igor drifted by, dry and not a hair out of place. "You all right?" he called out to us in a confident sort of manner!

"It'll be you next!" I yelled back.

The balsa rafts capsized many more times before we decided that it was safer if Dad, Malc and I walked round the most violent rapids. By lunchtime we came out of the worst section of the river and there seemed to be no sign of the others. What looked like Olaf's paddle came spinning into sight, followed by another pole. This did not bode well. Then Igor shot into sight, crouched low on his balsa. He saw us, paddled to the bank and lit a rare cigarette to calm his nerves.

"Olaf went first," he explained, "straight over the rock everyone was to avoid. I followed him, thinking he must know what he was doing . . . I just hope there's nothing more like that."

The other three arrived looking equally shattered. Olaf came out with his story in typically dramatic fashion. "My raft cartwheeled, I went down into the black and saw death. I thought of God and began to swim. I was dragged back under five times, each time I thought I would die."

The true heat of the afternoon was getting to us now, threatening to add sunburn to the insect bites, unsettled stomachs, and jungle heat lassitude. But the river began to change, becoming wider as we emerged from the gorge on to a broad plain and the rapids became gentler and less frequent. Abandoned chakras appeared on either bank and ahead huge snowy mountains forced their way high into the clear blue sky.

"Señorita." Olaf drew my attention. Although still stern, his eyes looked a little more friendly now. He nodded towards the right bank. "Villa Virgen," he said, and towards the left, "Lechemayo." It was Lechemayo that we were aiming for.

Along the bank were many families washing their clothes and bathing their pale jungle skin in the river. They waved at us, the children giggled as we passed. Most of these people would never have seen gringos before, and I could not help wondering how many of them would believe the Sendero stories about gringos kidnapping Indians and melting them down for the fine oil that is needed to lubricate hi-tech capitalist industrial machinery. As a metaphor it wasn't always that far from the truth.

Meanwhile, Dad was being met by the business end of a thirty-six-shot automatic rifle brandished by a young out-of-condition policeman, naked to the waist. Olaf was silent now, and we left the talking to Igor as we followed the hard-faced officer across the grassy plaza to the Guardia Civil post where the words "*Los Sinchis*" were painted in large letters across the front wall. We had not come across Los Sinchis before, and Igor explained that they had been the imperial guard of the Incas and were now the toughest commando unit of the Peruvian police.

As we walked into the building out of the bright sunlight, everything seemed black for a few moments. In the blackness I could hear the rough laughter of some of the police.

"Don't let's get locked up here, Dad," I said.

To our relief, the police captain was quite friendly. He was in his early thirties, a little lardy, but fit enough and though his eyes were now slow and gentle, I could see that on the job he would be ruthless. He introduced himself by his *nomme de guerre*, which was Gideon, warned us about the curfew and not drinking the water unpurified and said we could sleep in the school as there was a holiday at the moment. It was actually a national strike, lasting two weeks, to hinder the election of district mayors, so the school was not in use. We agreed to meet Olaf and the other two balseros for supper at the only café in the village. As we left the police barracks with Gideon, we could hear Olaf recounting stories of battles with Senderos to an appreciative audience. We all smiled at each other, glad he was being treated as the hero he was.

The school had a clean concrete floor and tin roof. We could wash out kit and dry it over the desks. The walls were painted white and, as well as the usual pictures of famous generals, supported two slogans which translated meant, "an open book is like a talking head" and "to arrive late is not to arrive." They were very keen on this sort of profound statement in the schools.

We ate an awful meal with Olaf and the other two, greasy pasta and hard-boiled plantains with warm beer and a soft drink that tasted like disinfectant. This was not the sort of farewell meal we had hoped to share with our three friends. As we talked around the grim plastic-coated table by the light of a candle, I thought how vulnerable Olaf and his friends looked without their weapons. I looked at Olaf; he was like a wild beast, I had never met anyone like him before, but I had never come across anyone who had to be like him. He seemed so cold and distant, as if these years of loneliness and struggle had moulded him into someone who could only survive by showing as little emotion as possible. It had been said that he had a wife and two sons, but where were they? There was no mention of them. This was Elizabeth's uncle, her blood. But he had not wanted to talk of Elizabeth.

Olaf told us how, in 1982, a road had been promised to cover the fifty miles from San Francisco to Villa Virgen across the river to get produce out to market. The Senderos persuaded the council not to go ahead with the project by hanging two of the village elders from the goalposts on the football pitch and stuffing their genitals in their mouths.

"This place is surrounded by the Senderos, it's completely cut off from the outside world. The only way in or out is by the river. It's all Narco country from here down to San Francisco, they control the coca farms back into the jungle on either side of the river. This is perfect coca-growing country. We have the Ronda and they have the Cumpas, their own groups of armed local men. They are far more aggressive than most Rondas, you'd best go downriver with the police if you possibly can."

With this severe warning given it was almost curfew, and we headed off our separate ways to bed. I wondered where Olaf would sleep tonight. Would he risk somebody's house?

Dad and Igor went with Olaf early the next morning to visit Villa Virgen. Malcolm and I said goodbye to him standing in the mud where we had arrived the day before. We shook hands, Olaf still did not look me in the eye. He stepped on to his raft and was gone. I felt overcome with sadness; what a lonely and bitter life, but how strong he had become through his adversity.

A lady teacher called Edna came to talk to us and sent her son round with a delicious meal of rice, fried yucca, tuna and bananas for us. The day got hotter and hotter, until all we could do was lie still on the floor of the school and sleep. Dad and Igor returned. They had been talking to Gideon and his second-in-command, Pinky, who had invited us all to lunch. Igor was going to try and get their radio going. It ran off solar power, of which there was no shortage, but it had broken down. Gideon and Pinky were hoping to confirm their posting out of Lechemayo. If Igor could fix the radio, then we could travel downriver with them. I hoped Igor could do his stuff.

The police ate well and even the fierce young man who had met us on the riverbank the day before was now all smiles. As we ate, another policeman was butchering mutton, his blood-stained apron tied tightly around an ample waist as he stretched the meat out and repeatedly brought down his heavy knife. Gideon explained that everyone had to have another job as well as being policemen, to keep their post going. There was not much for the police to do here, except play football when the heat allowed, but they claimed to have held off three hundred terrorists using slingshots of drink cans filled with explosives, nails, glass and excrement.

Malc surpassed himself in the eating stakes and took up the police challenge of seconds with gusto, but eventually we adjourned to the radio room, where Igor began to fiddle with knobs and wires. Pinky called, "*Colombia, Colombia, Colombia – Urano, Urano, Urano – Urgente, Urgente, Urgente,*" in a special radio voice over and over again. Gideon's parrot, a rather moth-eaten green object, walked backwards and forwards along the top of the door, screeching advice from time to time, most put out by all the toing and froing.

Just as Pinky was becoming hoarse and Igor was about to give up, a faint voice was heard over the airwaves: "*Urano, Urano – Colombia, Colombia.*" Gideon and Pinky were to leave with Apollo, an even tougher-looking specially trained bodyguard. We were to leave with them at dawn in two days' time.

We staggered back to the school to let our huge meal digest, and found Vlady, Edna's six-year-old son, leaning against the door shyly waiting for us with an invitation to supper and a lesson in chocolate-making. Maybe Don Pancho's promise of "bastante chocolate" was to come true at last.

Edna boosted the fire when we arrived at six o'clock and put a kilo of cocoa beans into a blackened cast-iron pot, stirring them with a stick until they were burnt black. The beans began to pop and the pot smoked. She tipped the hot beans on to a plate to cool and gave us some sort of fennel tea to drink, until they were cool enough for us to peel off the husks. Next the beans went into a cast-iron grinder, like the ones I remember Mum and Ada using before the electricity came. Two spoons of beans were added to one of crude cane sugar. Worms of almost liquid chocolate appeared, rich with the cocoa butter still intact.

My appetite was beginning to return. I love chocolate. Water was put on to boil with a piece of cinnamon stick to add that something special, then we mixed in the chocolate paste with tinned milk to taste. It was delicious, but terribly rich. Little Vlady and I had become quite good friends through sign language, and while the chocolate-tasting was going on, he crept up behind me and shoved something in my mouth. I chewed and swallowed, obediently. It was really quite tasteless, I said, wondering what I had been fed. A fat yellow fly, according to Dad and Malcolm, who would not try one.

The villagers brought nicer gifts of pineapples, bananas and avocados over the next couple of days, and in the evening darkness we would sit on the concrete step outside the school and sing with them, taking it in turns with one of theirs, one of ours. We talked and worried about what was in store for us as we travelled downriver into the heart of terrorism and the drug trade. Dad was genning us up on one-to-one confrontation. But I felt there was little chance of me overpowering anyone, and my best hope was to be taken captive. For ransom or for breeding? My imagination ran riot.

After a restless night came the day we were to leave Lechemayo and travel downstream in the dug-out police canoe to San Pancho, as they called San Francisco locally. We packed up and made our way to Juan Jorge's shop for the "expresso" ride. Juan Jorge was a small fat slob of a man, commonly known to make his ample living from ferrying sacks of coca leaves downriver for the Narcos and bringing stores back upstream for his shop, which was little more than a front. Whether the police could not or dare not pin anything on him I am not sure. We waited the whole afternoon for Juan Jorge to return. When darkness fell, we gave up and went back to the school. Gideon was furious and embarrassed by the failure of the arrangement which was set up again for the following morning.

So we made our way down to the river again through the first hint of dawn. Remarkably, there was the dug-out canoe, approximately thirty feet long, the lower part dug out of a single native hardwood tree, called *cedro*, the sides built up with planks. At the stern were two rather tatty-looking forty-horse-power outboards. Altogether it did not inspire much confidence – it could be quite a trip ahead.

Although the police had hired the canoe, it was also loaded with twenty huge sacks of cocoa beans, two wild piglets and Gideon's parrot who slipped and fluttered into the river. He looked more awful than usual when scooped out, with his feathers stuck to his scrawny body, screeching abuse to restore his dignity.

We finally departed on the "expresso" trip at 6.20 a.m. The police were dressed in civilian clothes, but heavily armed. Hand grenades were passed around and Dad was given a pump-action shotgun. One of the policemen had to bail with a bucket all the time.

We passed San Antonio at speed, watched by armed men from the riverbank. Now the houses were built on stilts. Sometimes the river narrowed and the canoe had to slow to navigate rapids and rocks. Everyone scanned the tree-lined banks, for these were the places where the Senderos would wait in ambush. Weapons were cocked but kept out of sight. I found myself loving the excitement, and I knew the others did too. Our canoe was well loaded and deep in the water, so it was not long before we were aground and had to get out while the pilot and Juan Jorge pushed and pulled it into deeper waters where we could all get back in.

Now the land flattened out on both sides of the river into perfect coca-growing country. A kilo of leaves, made into coca paste and refined, produces one gram of cocaine. We passed a low island in the river, which Gideon explained had a landing-strip on it for light aircraft. Wreckage strewn along the beach was evidence of expensive miscalculations by the drug-traffickers.

Huge plumes of black smoke were rising into the sky, evidence of more jungle being cleared for the production of cocaine.

The "catfish row" town, as Dad remembered San Pancho, came into sight at 11.30 a.m., the main part sprawling and tin roofed on the left bank, but this was the first bridge over the Apurimac which vehicles could cross, and was generally considered the highest navigable point of the river. The bridge was of massive box-section steel construction, much larger than I had expected and brown with rust.

I I

Death Zone

The troops manning the river-control post were serious soldiers, wearing bulletproof vests, with webbing over the top, sporting anti-personnel rockets and grenades. Their FAL self-loading rifles with butts folded carried two magazines taped end to end for double firepower. We all perked up dramatically with the contagious vitality that came from these young men, and I felt my flowery skirt distinctly out of place.

Gideon's word cleared us, apart from a brief look at our passports.

"No photographs beyond this point," snapped the sergeant.

Six soldiers appeared on the concrete to escort us up a flight of steps that led from the landing-stage to the marine headquarters.

"You and the señorita keep to the left," the sergeant barked at Dad, "and the other two to the right." Igor and Malcolm were almost standing to attention in their eagerness not to get out of line. "Move quickly from doorway to doorway, you may be fired on from windows above." The patrol began to move, and we rushed to keep up, breathing hard under the weight of our packs in the midday heat.

At the top of the steps, we reached a dirt track which was the main road through the town and down to the bridge. We passed an open grassy verge with a sign that warned, "*Zona Minada Peligro*", but there was no fence to keep people or animals out. Here, at a T-junction in the track, was the headquarters of the Marina Infantaria and the one rooming-house, the Hostal Suria, where we would stay for our safety. It also housed many of the police.

We returned to the barracks at the double, having been told, "The captain is a very difficult man, he does not like to be kept waiting." But it was the petty officer who inspected our papers after advising us calmly, "Please move to the other side of the doorway." Glancing just above Malcolm's head, he explained, "That chip out of the concrete was made by a machine-gun bullet yesterday. It came from somewhere on the hill, over there. Another bullet went through the camouflage netting above us, through the side of a seventeen-year-old soldier who was getting dressed to come on duty. He is dead."

There had been more deaths than usual recently, some to do with the municipal elections, but it was a good muddled time to settle old scores.

"In the past five days, fifty people have been killed in this town, and there have been at least fourteen deaths along the river between Lechemayo and here," a handsome young lieutenant volunteered. "Just before you arrived, three bodies were brought down by canoe."

Sounding suitably demure, Igor said that we were sorry to be in the way, and would leave as soon as we could get on a convoy to Ayacucho, now that the national strike was over. The lieutenant promised to see what he could do, but it would depend on whether Ayacucho were willing to accept us, and meanwhile we must hand over our passports and not leave the *hostal*.

No foreigners had been here for at least eight years, journalists were murdered, and the outside world did not know what went on in such cut-off and beleaguered places as San Francisco. From our window we could watch what passed by in the street below and also view the goings-on behind a high wall which separated the military compound from the street. For a while we were joined by a group of off-duty policemen slouched on the second-floor balcony. Dad advised us to sit back in the shadows, as we were a perfect target for sniper fire.

Our three Sinchi friends returned in high spirits from their debriefing with hopes of an early police convoy to Ayacucho. Gideon was pretty sure we would be allowed to travel on with them, but worried for our safety. The Senderos would know we were here and to take or kill us would be perfect international publicity for them.

A battered Mercedes truck roared out of the barracks towards the river. There had been a tip-off that a Colombian plane was going to land somewhere in the area to pick up five hundred kilos of coca paste. But the policemen shrugged, saying it was almost impossible for the soldiers to guess which landing-strip it would use and there were not enough patrols to cover them all. Not long ago a plane had landed at the strip just across the river, picked up its cargo and taken off again before a patrol could get across the bridge.

Death Zone

By late afternoon the first body was carried down the street, wrapped in a blanket and held high. The widow followed beating her hands together in sorrow and the mourners made angry gestures towards the barracks for being unable to protect life. The day's traffic that had braved the road from Ayacucho began to arrive in convoy and with it the depressing news that the police relief had not set off. We would not be able to leave next morning. As light faded more bodies were carried along the street.

In the evening we were allowed out to get a meal and a local bank clerk took Gideon, Pinky, Apollo and us four to a tiny dive with cartoons painted on the wall. Dad brought along our emergency bottle of Johnnie Walker to celebrate our being alive this far. We were all in high spirits. The hyped-up mood of the marines at the barracks who diced with death every day had got our own adrenalin pumping round like mad. Dad was, of course, in his element. Malc was seeing a life not likely to have been experienced by any other of his Sandhurst intake a few months on, Igor was enjoying the wheeler-dealing of being our chief negotiator and I, my Spanish improving in leaps and bounds, was somewhat to Dad's alarm getting hooked on the excitement of everything.

We drank beer with our chicken and rice, after which Dad passed round drams and talked through a plan of action if we were ambushed. We would dive for cover and throw bottles, while the Sinchis opened fire, except Apollo who was so drunk he fell off his chair backwards, at which point we decided to call it a day before the 9 p.m. curfew.

While I was snatching a rare chance of the shower working, there came a knock at the door and Igor passed on a sobering story. One of the last trucks coming through from Ayacucho had been stopped at a road block at a place called Monte Rio, everyone was lined up at the side of the road, and six of the men shot in the back of the head.

The next day it did not look as though we were going to be allowed to go anywhere, and it passed much as the day before. Patrols came and went. Bodies were carried down the street in blankets. Pinky got drunk. The following day was the same. Looking out from our room over into the barracks compound we saw seven handcuffed men facing the wall with their shirts tied over their heads. While a lieutenant was haranguing them, the captain looked up and angrily spotted us watching. I backed off. Dad didn't. Later in the afternoon all seven were released.

105

I wondered whether their fate might have been different if we had not been unwanted witnesses.

At last two armour-plated open trucks built in Israel roared in. This was the police escort to take us to Ayacucho, the town whose Quechua name means Corner of the Dead.

We got up in a rush next morning, Pinky waving at us to hurry from the street below as the trucks were loading at 5.30 a.m. Gideon sat in the front passenger seat, the one they called the death seat. In the back we perched on unpadded metal benches facing outwards. Next to me on one side was a Sinchi wife who had travelled from Lechemayo with us. She was thrilled at the next step in her travels back to "civilisation", but hissed and spat about the discomfort. Dad sat on the other side of me, nearest the tailgate, and had a small murderess put on his knee by the police guard of San Francisco. She was being sent for trial and looked tough and angry at all the fuss. With the traditional long plaits tied together at the end, full skirt, clean blouse and bright pink cardigan, she looked pretty switched-on to me. A small child, whether hers or a grandchild I do not know, perched on her knee, playing with a razor blade, with no dissuasion from her. Maybe she was a murderess? She had no conversation and spared us not even a glance.

Our convoy of four was led by the marine captain in a Mercedes truck, and on his word, all four engines roared into life and we took off at breakneck speed along the twisting dirt road that climbed out of the valley. We would rise from 1500 feet out of the steaming secondary tangle of jungle that provided such good cover for the Senderos, to a height of 14,000 feet and back down again to around 8000 in the dustbowl of Ayacucho.

We scanned the jungle as we hurtled on, occasionally coming to burnt-out shells of houses next to their chakras of abandoned crops. We all felt nervous; not only was there the danger from a terrorist ambush, but the prospect of meeting on-coming traffic was an added worry. The hillside dropped away steeply and the Senderos had made so many boulder road blocks that the road was mostly only open to one vehicle width.

After a relatively short time, the convoy came to a sudden screeching stop and the marines from the two Mercedes jumped out, moving up the breadth of the road on foot to test for mines. The marine captain waited, recklessly we thought, in the front of his Mercedes, drumming his fingers on the top of the windscreen. Was he not a perfect target for ambush? All was well and we sped off again.

In the elbow of the next bend, our marine escort left us close to a burnt-out house which looked as if it had recently been the scene of bloodshed. He waved us through and turned back to his truck. Now we were one less problem for him to deal with. Police and marines exchanged good-natured insults and brandished their weapons in parting.

Malcolm's bowels took the moment to demand his undivided attention on the way to a place called Tambo.

"This is serious!" Malc said. "You'll have to get them to stop."

"There is no way they will stop, Malc," replied Igor. "They can't risk us all getting killed, you'll have to go off the back."

"This is seriously embarrassing," said poor Malc, as he moved towards the back of the lurching truck. What made it worse was that we were the front truck. Dad said that he saw the truck behind start up its windscreen wipers, but I think he was exaggerating. The Sinchi wife next to me was appalled, but the men were all laughing. Pinky told Malc that he was part way to becoming a Sinchi himself, for Pinky had had to swim across a tank of human excrement during his training.

Up on to the dry, bleached altiplano, our bones rattled as we bumped along, and we were covered in a fine dust, like theatrical ageing powder. After almost five hours we reached Tambo. The murderess was led away and we were told that there would be an hour-long meal stop. We were pleased to find that when Olaf's name was mentioned to the intelligence officer making heavy weather of our papers his mood completely changed. Olaf was held in high regard by the military chiefs of Ayacucho, he assured us.

The Sinchi drivers did not slow at all as we swung round the hairpins, climbing out of the high valley on the next leg of our journey. We travelled second now. The first truck ground to a halt with a puncture and there were angry words between Gideon and his colleague as the wheel was changed. The gap between us widened. Eventually we reached the high pass, and began our descent across the dusty plains to Ayacucho, where we came upon the first truck again with another puncture. This time the mean-faced older Sinchi captain commandeered our truck to go for a spare wheel, leaving us a sitting target on the side of the road. Gideon was furious. Pinky, Apollo and the driver were not too thrilled either. Gideon handed Dad a pump-action shot-gun, and told us all to spread out.

Two young men appeared in the distance, walking towards us. Pinky ordered them to stop, lay out the contents of their bag on the road and show their papers. What were they doing here, in what seemed like the middle of nowhere? They said that they had been playing in a football match at the next village, but because of the oncoming thunderstorm, the match had been called off. Gideon told them to be on their way, and we watched anxiously as they walked away.

Igor went off in search of cactus fruit, which we peeled carefully to avoid the prickles. The coccus insect which lives on these cactus is collected and crushed, its scarlet blood making the red dye, cochineal. Tremendous fork lightning now cut the purple sky. Our situation was not getting any better. Pinky was cheerful, teasing Malc as usual, Gideon was still angry, Apollo remained strong and silent. The driver stayed close to the vehicle, still looking embarrassed. When heavy rain began to fall, we sheltered under the vehicle for a while but, after another truck passed, we went back to being spread out and got wet instead.

It was two hours before the relief truck arrived, the wheel was changed and we were off again at full tick, the parrot clinging to Gideon up front, while we swerved this way and that to avoid the boulders. Houses along the roadside became more frequent as we neared Ayacucho, the birthplace of the Sendero Luminoso, with its seventy-five thousand desperately poor inhabitants.

It was almost dark as we stopped outside the smart Hotel Turistica. It looked a real money-grabber, not quite our usual choice, but Gideon said he had been ordered to "release" us at a hotel with a permanent military guard. This was it. We were very sad to leave Gideon, Pinky and Apollo, and after warm Latin American embraces, we stood on the side of the road waving as the truck sped away into the darkness. Only Pinky's final taunt to Malc could be heard above the engine. "*Malcong, maldito soldat! Lost terrucas . . .*" as he drew his hand across his throat.

Inside the enormous hotel the smart uniformed staff rather looked down their noses at our dusty travel-stained party, perhaps half-wondering if we could pay. The place seemed deserted, apart from a few Peruvians in tracksuits on a sports convention and a pair of white mountain foxes who prowled round and round their glass prison. Long gone were the rich American tourists who used to throng here. The hot intermittent showers and a bed with sheets were the creature comforts I had sometimes longed for, but now I was already missing the simple life and the real people.

We had found Olaf, tested ourselves both mentally and physically and experienced a harsh, different way of life. There were many tales to tell Elizabeth when she wanted to know.

12

Natural Family

With Phase One complete, we could begin the second leg of our journey which would take us back to Accobamba where we had first met Elizabeth four years earlier. We hoped her natural mother, Leocadia, and grandparents Josephina and Juan Huaman were still there. We wanted to take news of Elizabeth to them and get news of them for Elizabeth. Through Malcolm's father, a doctor, we had also managed to get hold of some hearing aids, and hoped we could help Leocadia's deafness.

We were now in a very much weakened state. Igor had to go back to work in Lima, leaving Dad, Malcolm and me to survive with our smattering of Spanish and friendly smiles. But Malcolm was a shadow of his former self, a Samson who had lost all his strength, without the snip of a scissors, brought to his knees by desperate stomach problems. After a bad night at the Turistica Hotel I knew I was rapidly joining Malc's condition. Could we really have amoebic dysentery? I had heard people talk of it before, but always thought they were exaggerating. Luckily, Dad seemed to be all right, except for his bad knee.

We flew from Ayacucho to Cuzco early the next morning, for a moment lulled by the comfort of air travel and spectacular views of jagged snow-covered peaks piercing the sky below. At Cuzco Igor waved goodbye from the steps of the jet which would take him on to the comfort of Lima. For our part we must now move slowly, so as not to succumb to the well known *soroche*, the throbbing headache of altitude sickness. Fortunately for our enfeebled state the next stage of the journey would demand no more than surviving a Peruvian train ride, down into the jungle and back to Quillabamba, the end of the line. Malc and I only just managing to keep going. We knew we must drink plenty to keep our fluids up, and eat, but felt like neither. My plaited leather belt is so useful in these "slim fast" situations, it fits me whatever size I am; but the tail was getting longer each day.

On the train at mid-day I felt a little better, though I was keen not to visit the loo which became foul after the first hour of the journey, and I hung on to my loo paper with the same keenness as my passport. A plump American woman sat opposite, chatting to Dad and passing round Sun Maid Raisins in their small red boxes; they must be safe to eat. The air became humid as we zig-zagged down steep mountainsides after losing all other white faces at the stop for Machu Pichu. The carriage had now filled with large Quechua women carrying great bundles of wares tied up in wide squares of cloth. These were the traders who take baskets of jungle fruits up to Cuzco at 12,000 feet and bring back clothes and other goods from the outside world to sell to the people of the jungle. Other women hawked plates of stew loudly through the carriage, turning my stomach as they did so with these killer meals.

We spent the night at Quillabamba before getting a truck on. The proprietress of the local *hostal* asked how Elizabeth was. This was the first place my sister saw electric light and slept in a bed, but she had still squatted naturally in the courtyard as she had not seen a loo before. Malc and I chewed determinedly on dry bread and drank fizzy bottled water before getting onto a truck going to Yupanca. I was, if anything, feeling worse, but knew that if we kept going, we could rest in Padre Santiago's room off the church at Pucyura. The truck driver saw how ill I was and let me sit in the cab next to his wife, saving me from the scorching sun, dust and discomfort in the back. The six-hour bumpy, uphill journey seemed to go on for ever, and I was dreading the moment when I would have to ask the driver to stop so that I could rush off into the bushes. But due to us having eaten so little, this problem did not occur. Malc and I were pretty quick to make the most of all proper stops.

The truck was going no further than Yupanca. We ate rice and stayed in a flea-pit for the night. Morale was low. Self-pity swept over me and I sobbed briefly in my sleeping bag, then felt much better. In the morning we walked up the dirt track to Pucyura carrying all our kit. I felt weak, as if my head was not connected to my body, but I kept moving forward. Malc was in a much worse state than me, having to stop every few steps. "I just can't believe where my strength has gone," he moaned in his soft Scottish tones.

After three days' rest in Padre Santiago's cool, quiet, white-washed room we were stronger and ready to go. Roberto was again to be our guide, with a rather unpleasant younger companion, Arturo. We had arranged to hire three horses and a mule. I was to ride the small horse, Dad and Malc were to take it in turns to ride the larger one. Neither of them were very keen horsemen. Malc had spent a lot of his childhood on his uncle's farm where, though there were no horses, he somehow felt the farming part would stand him in good stead. The other horse and mule were to carry the kit and food. After four shortish walking days, Malc had been kicked by one of the horses and Dad was thrown off by the other, narrowly missing a drop of hundreds of feet down the mountain side, and badly injuring his ribs and leg. We had battled across the Abra Huamas in snow at 16,500 feet, with the sound of avalanches crashing all around us in the clouds, and dropped down slowly into verdant areas, arriving at last at Accobamba.

As we walked through the scattering of houses that make up the village, a gentle breeze cooled our tired bodies, and rustled the leaves of the great eucalyptus trees bordering the Inca Highway. We passed the house where Mum and I had drunk coffee with the crippled woman, Birginie, four years previously and first learnt of Elizabeth's existence. It seemed as if we had been here only yesterday, I remembered it so vividly. So much had happened in Elizabeth's life, the time had flashed past.

Now I found I was quite nervous at meeting Elizabeth's natural family again. Maybe they would say that they wanted her back, maybe they would think we had come with bad news. We were all a bit fraught, Dad calling me "Rebecca" instead of "Bec", which usually means trouble.

As we walked round the corner of the house we had been directed to, there were Leocadia and Josephina sitting in the shade, next to a large poncho covered with haricot-vert, drying in the sun. They recognised us instantly, smiled at each other, and got to their short square feet. I remembered how small they were, only coming up to my chest. We hugged each other, and although there was no common language, our smiles and gestures were ample. We soon found ourselves sitting on sheepskins in the shade, sipping strong sweet coffee from bashed enamel mugs, and eating boiled new potatoes. How strange it was to be at Accobamba, inexorably linked to these almost stone age people, Elizabeth our common bond.

Later, as darkness dropped its inky curtain around us, Juan Huaman returned from his day's work in the chakra further down the valley. He carried a simple short-handled digging tool over one shoulder and his other bits and pieces in a *manta* round his waist, spun and woven by his wife from their own wool and dyed dark brown with the bark from the tree in front of their house. I admired their ingenuity. Every possession they had was crude and usually home-made, but for a special task. I thought of the clutter that I had accumulated already. Was it all really necessary? I used the excuse that because we lived in such a remote place, we had to hang on to everything in case one day it would be needed. Justin used to throw things away when I was not looking, but I would rescue them from the rubbish before I burnt it. Now I felt romantically I would like to live this simple life and remove myself from materialism.

Roberto and Arturo seemed to consume at least double the amount of potatoes that any of us could. My appetite was returning slowly, but I could not keep anything in my stomach for very long. In Dad's small shaving mirror, my face looked thinner than ever and my eyes were sinking back, my hair was also coming out in alarming quantities when I washed it. Malc looked very thin too, he was still weakened but his gargantuan appetite was returning. Dad for his part was still in great pain from the fall that had damaged his ribs and took arnica for his injury.

We tried to converse through Roberto, who could translate our poor Spanish into Quechua, but this made for very stilted conversation. Dad persevered to glean facts to pass on to Elizabeth in his meticulous way, but I was quite happy to read what I could from their expressions and actions. I crawled in through the small doorway of the cook house to be in the women's domain. At this altitude guests eat outside, higher up where the weather is colder, they are called inside at the last minute to eat. The cooking ritual seemed to be kept private, between women or women and children. It was everyday details like this that I wanted to observe, just as they watched with wonderment our fanatical body and clothes washing.

There was an embarrassed giggle from Leocadia as my lanky frame insinuated itself into the mud-walled room. The glowing wood fire highlighted the deepening leathery lines of Josephina's familiar worried expression. Leocadia's expression was very different. In her mid-thirties, her face was still childlike, her skin soft and relatively unaged, only small lines appeared on either side of her nose, when she smiled or laughed. I could see Elizabeth in her so strongly, in the way she moved, the way she breathed and looked embarrassed when she noticed me watching her, the expression in her eyes, the shy smile and endearing crinkly nose; although mother and daughter had been apart for over three years, their mannerisms were still the same.

I watched the two women prepare a large pot of potato soup and a separate one of boiled potatoes, using their one sharp knife with its melted plastic handle and blade worn in a narrow curve. Leocadia fetched water, washed the potatoes and got the fire burning hot, by blowing down a piece of charred bamboo into the embers. Josephina seemed quite impatient with her daughter, scowling from time to time, but Leocadia paid little attention and continued to smile shyly at me, just as Elizabeth did. As I watched it became more and more apparent that Leocadia really could not look after herself, let alone a child. She helped, but she was being directed by her mother. It was hard to imagine how she could get by in this harsh world without being protected from reality. Then there was her deafness. It was difficult to tell how much she could hear, or maybe she lip-read. Her speech could only be understood by her parents and those who knew her well. The family seemed pretty well set up now, with plenty of guinea pigs scurrying across the floor, eating the greenery put down for them, and outside some hens, pigs, piglets and four scrawny sheep.

After eating our supper, where it seemed polite to slurp your soup, we retired to lay out our bivvy bags on top of some sheepskins on the mud porch. Mother, father and daughter watched and giggled as we undressed in the dark. I had become quite proficient at this and was soon pushing my toes into the corners of my sleeping-bag liner, jumping up and down to pull it up to my neck, which caused great mirth. I felt the ice was now truly broken.

Our hosts were up before the dawn, and Choquesapra's ice-capped peak looked sharp and close in the bright morning sun, which had not yet filled the valley when we awoke, our bodies covered with many flea-bites from the sheepskins. After breakfast of coffee and potatoes, I got out the small presents I had brought from home: a selection of Suttons seeds for Juan Huaman, carrots, onions, tomatoes, beetroot, celery, courgettes, aubergines and a few flowers. In this rich soil and fantastic growing climate, I hoped most would flourish, though I expected he would think the flowers a bit of a waste of time where everything is grown for a purpose. For Josephina and Leocadia I had large square cotton scarves, one red, the other with big pink flowers and brilliant green leaves, and velvet bows on hair clips to match each. There were lots of photographs of Elizabeth, which they looked at over and over again, commenting on how she had grown, how she wore her hair, what lovely clothes she had and how plump and healthy she looked. Dad gave Juan Huaman a storm lantern, too, which we had bought in Quillabamba.

Leocadia and Josephina were thrilled with their scarves and hair clips, draping the scarves round their heads and shoulders in as many different ways as they could think of. This was the first time I had really seen Josephina laugh. I clipped the luxurious bows at the end of their thick long black plaits, which they swung over their shoulders so they could see how fine they looked. Women were always asking me for my hair clip which was just a plastic tortoiseshell one. Velvet bows were far superior. There were hugs and "*Gracias Mammita*" over and over.

We then got the hearing aids out, to see if they could help Leocadia. It was going to be difficult to explain with the language barrier and the deafness. Sign language seemed the only thing. I was very excited, hoping that this could change Leocadia's life for the better, but did she really understand what the hearing aid was? I did not believe that she did, and I do not think that Josephina or Juan Huaman really understood either. Again, through Roberto, we tried to explain what this thing could do, but it must have seemed so remarkable and unbelievable. Leocadia was fairly keen to try it, but there was little encouragement from her parents, and little change of expression in her glazed eyes when she did so. I left her to try it out, but later in the day there was no sign of it.

Juan Huaman cut the throat of one of his four sheep in honour of our visit. I then helped to skin and gut the pitifully small creature before its scrawny carcass was taken to the cook house, hacked into pieces and hung in the smoke. Everything was saved, and later in the day we ate bowlfuls of acidic intestines and tripe. Malc and I could not eat very much of this delicacy and fed most of ours to the starving flea-ridden puppy under the table, the darkness hiding our terrible deed.

The next morning, after visiting the Inca ruins on the hillside over-looking Accobamba, we had to begin our journey home. Juan Huaman and Josephina sent messages to Elizabeth of love and urged her to make the most of the opportunity she had been given. I felt satisfied that what we had been asked to do and what we had done was the right thing. Elizabeth is loved dearly by us and many others, she is happy and has the chance to grow beyond what she could possibly have if left where she was. She can always return, when she has made the most of her opportunity, one hopes perhaps to help her fellow countrymen.

I was choked by emotion as I hugged her mother and grandparents. Would we ever see them again? They were very frightened that the terrorists were advancing again, the trouble was not over. Round the end of the house, and up on to the path, I turned for the last time. The solitary figure of Leocadia stood separate from the house, calling "*Caio*" in her difficult way. She waved and smiled, seemingly unaffected by our departure. Although it was Leocadia standing there, through my tears, all I could see was Elizabeth.

Part Three

CAPE HORN

13

Something Amazing

It was a blustery day in late April 1990, the harshness of winter was over and the twenty-second season of the John Ridgway Adventure School was in full swing. I had been testing my cooking skills on the Instructors' course, and now I was helping Mum with the office work, as well as instructing on the Businessmen's courses. Four months had passed since I had waved goodbye to Leocadia. Justin was off on his run in the Himalayas and Jon Williams had taken over from him as chief instructor and skipper of *English Rose VI*. He was doing a good job, and we were already keen for him to stay on for the next season. But JW was someone who liked to move on to fresh challenges. At present he was sitting at the kitchen table up in the croft in his usual navy blue Helly Hansen fibre pile top and blue tracksters, his neatly trimmed gingery beard moving to the rhythm of his jaws as he concentrated on a sandwich.

"What are you thinking of doing this winter, JW?" asked Mum.

JW looked seriously down at his sandwiches, through round glasses. It was always the same. Had he heard the question?

"Well, first I'm going to visit Julie in Japan, and then I'd really like to do some ice climbing." His mind appeared to have drifted off, before he added, "But then I would like to do some more canoeing, too."

"Why don't you and John go off and do that trip Jamie Young did? Canoeing round Cape Horn, wasn't it? He could give you some tips. You ought to get in touch with him, Johnnie," suggested Mum. But she was more interested in finishing off the lunch break, and getting back to the office. "Would you like tea or coffee, John? Johnnie . . . tea or coffee? It's so infuriating, when you don't answer!"

"Coffee, please," Dad replied, but he was already miles away in tempestuous albatross seas. For he had sailed *English Rose VI* twice round Cape Horn and he'd even been on Cape Horn island the previous January with Igor, doing a recce for a BBC film. Here was a good idea. At least canoeing wouldn't affect his knees too much, which were still playing up after his fall from the horse in Peru.

At this time of year the south-westerly storms die away, and there are often days of gentle easterlies. The wind blows off the land and the swell is deadened; sun shines and rain stops – conditions are perfect for everything but sailing. Come the first available day like this, Dad and JW pushed off from the rocky shore in their fragile craft, Dad was paddling an orange Nordkapp kayak which had been dusted down after some years of storage in the workshop roof. It had belonged to an instructor who had paddled it down the west coast of Alaska. While he was at Ardmore, an ultimatum was issued by his girlfriend: "It's me or the job." Struggling to come to terms with having his wings clipped, the poor fellow wrote off his Mini; with no finances and no car, the beloved kayak had to be abandoned – we hoped the romance blossomed. JW paddled an old white touring kayak which had once been used for instructional purposes but had lain dormant on the back of the canoe rack for some years.

They paddled out along the north shore of Loch Laxford to the open sea, round Ardmore point and across Loch Dughaill, on their way up the west coast to rendezvous with the course of businessmen beneath the cliffs at the mouth of Loch an Roin. These brave souls had either orienteered out to this empty place or got there by paddling their light and very stable plastic kayaks across a chain of fresh-water lochs.

Even though the wind was blowing off the shore, it was quite choppy at the mouth of the sea lochs, and Dad had capsized twice by the time he and JW met up with the course for lunch. Without a wet suit, and with the water still not that much above freezing, he'd been fairly close to his limits and had got a realistic view of what was involved in the notion of canoeing round Cape Horn. The whole sea kayaking game was not quite as easy as it had seemed sitting by the kitchen table. JW thought Dad would quit.

I listened to Dad's story while he lay in the bath letting the warmth soak into his back. But I could tell sea kayaking had gripped him and, once keen on something, Dad is totally single-minded. I too, had to admit to that familiar bubbling feeling of excitement deep in my stomach while I listened to the adventure he and JW had just had.

"How would you like to be the first girl to canoe round Cape Horn?" grinned my father.

There was a pause.

"Do you really think I could do it?" The image my mind's eye conjured up frightened me. Maybe this was half the pull.

"Yeah, 'course you could!" Dad replied.

I did not want to say yes or no, just like that, but I felt this could be what I had been looking for: it would indeed be something amazing.

JW had learned to canoe at school and university, he was good and safe. Dad had done quite a bit in the army, the Devizes to Westminster race a couple of times, and of course at Ardmore. I had been introduced to it at the age of eight when I invited my two best friends from school in Kinlochbervie out for the day, and we joined in with one of the groups of young people. Fiona and I leapt into the last free double canoe, leaving poor Angela, who was not suited to the outdoor life, to wrestle with a single on her own. The day was not a conspicuous social success, and we ended up with blistered thumbs and aching arms from trying to keep up with people bigger than ourselves. I did not like this much. I did some more canoeing in my sixth form but all in the school swimming pool, where most of the session was spent swimming under the water while still in the canoe and then pulling myself upright on the side of the pool: I had enjoyed this even less. Now, back at Ardmore, I had begun to enjoy it a lot more in the sheltered sea lochs. Finding I was not the worst helped, and I was soon able to teach others the basic skills while beginners' fears were still very real to me. But I hadn't done any sea kayaking, so I would be learning those skills from scratch, with the goal of facing the ultimate challenge.

We now had to find someone to teach us. It is one thing to paddle round a sheltered sea loch in a short stable plastic canoe, where going in a straight line might be your greatest worry, but an 18-foot narrow fibreglass sea kayak in the turbulent waters where ocean meets land is quite different. The word "commitment" seems to crop up quite often.

How could my weedy thin arms and body ever become strong enough to battle against strong winds for hours on end?

Dad phoned Jamie Young, who'd been an instructor for many of the early years at Ardmore. I remembered him as a stalwart member of the crew on *English Rose V*, when we sailed to the Spanish Sahara when I was only seven years old. He and his wife, Mary, whom he'd met at

Ardmore, now ran their own adventure school on the west coast of Ireland. Jamie's report on his three-man trip to Cape Horn in 1988 made scary reading. As far as we could tell this was only the second team ever to try the trip, and on his advice we got in touch with Frank Goodman who had led the four Britons who had been the first ever to kayak round Cape Horn, back in 1977.

Frank Goodman recommended Nigel Dennis as an excellent teacher; in 1980, he had been the first man to canoe round Great Britain. Now he ran his own school in Anglesey, specialising in sea kayaking. Nigel agreed to come up to Ardmore in early July 1990 and, in the meantime, we pored over the expedition reports, charts and suppliers of kayaks and kit.

Dad described the Cape Horn summer as being similar to our north Highland winter, just a succession of depressions; the difference being that while at Cape Wrath we might get one or two lows a week, around Cape Horn we could expect one or more a day. The weather would be difficult to predict, and only one misjudgement could be the end of us.

After successfully circumnavigating the Horn, Jamie's team faced near disaster on the return journey, which seemed to bear out Dad's old saying that many more soldiers are killed while returning from patrols to enemy lines than are ever lost on the way out. It seems that on one wild night, while camped on a small island among the Wollaston group, just north of the Horn, Jamie's team had one of their three kayaks washed away by an exceptional diurnal variation in the tide, caused by storm surge. The owner of the missing kayak became consumed with guilt. After searching the coastline with his tent-mate for three hours in the dark, the predicament overwhelmed him. He set off alone in one of the two remaining kayaks, leaving his two companions asleep. Crossing the channel to a neighbouring island, he doggedly continued hunting until he did at last find his kayak. But the wind had now risen to Force Ten and he could not possibly tow the fragile shell back across the channel.

When daylight came his two friends were able to pick him out with binoculars on the distant shore, slithering about among the kelp, and they knew he had neither sleeping bag nor food and that he must be cold and nearly done for. By late afternoon, fearing their friend would be stranded, Jamie's companion set off in what was still appalling weather, taking kit for the two of them to survive the night, and leaving

Jamie very literally marooned on his island to watch helplessly as his two friends, testing themselves beyond previously conceived limits, struggled back across the wild channel with the three kayaks.

Reading that report over and over again, I realised just how easy it is to make a rash decision when feelings are dramatically heightened by an all-consuming desire to succeed. We mustn't allow it to happen to us.

After Nigel's first visit it was decided that we should postpone the trip for a year; it was foolhardy to think we could gain enough skill and experience in four months, when most of our time was needed for the Adventure School anyway. But Nigel was keen to join the team himself and he agreed to train us. By postponing the trip until December 1991 we could become much more proficient. The winter of 1990 would prove invaluable for training at home in the north of Scotland and at Nigel's school in Anglesey.

Thousands of people have attended courses at Ardmore over the past twenty years and many have become firm friends. A wiry Scot called David Dey has battled it out with Dad on the morning run for more than two decades. David was now a main board director of British Telecom and he saw the kayak expedition as an opportunity for very practical testing of a new satellite communication system that they were developing. We were to have a BT Research Engineer with us on the trip. I hoped to send a signal from my kayak off Cape Horn to a satellite 11,000 miles above. From there my message would pass through a land station in Denmark, across to the UK, and eventually via a cable, under the loch and up the hill into a telex printer in the house. Mum would always know where I was, and she could let Dad know the daily feed-rates on the salmon farm.

Mike Hay, a stalwart from what used to be Rhodesia, and managing director of Survival Anglia, had also been on many courses at Ardmore. Now he set about planning the first professional film ever made on a sea kayaking expedition. Jack Tolson was to be director/cameraman on the trip.

From the bottom of a trench in Daharan, as Saddam Hussein's SCUD missiles began their fatal descent, ITN producer Bill Taylor thought his end might be nigh, and promised himself a return visit to the tranquillity of a canoe on Loch Laxford if he survived. And it came to pass that Bill did survive and, seated in a canoe once more, which he found more frightening than the SCUDs, he conceived the idea of regular film reports to ITN each night from a kayak off Cape Horn. Which was how John Boyce found himself aiming his camera at me from the front of a double kayak.

"John, get your fat ass down there!" would bellow the ebullient Norman Chambers, American chief executive of Rockwater, world leader in underwater engineering, for whom we had run several team-building courses. Letting us name the kayaks *Rockwater 1–7* took strong nerves: who wanted to see their name stuck on a kayak sinking on television? But if we succeeded . . .

Dad has great skill at organising expeditions and keeping all interested parties deployed. He makes meticulous records of every telephone call made, every detail discussed, right down to the most minute piece of information: nothing is left to chance. I have never met anyone remotely like him, thank God. Soon the kit was piling up in the workshop down by the sea at the foot of the croft, and we now had a much larger team. First it had been just Dad and JW, but then I was added. Then came Nigel Dennis and Aled Williams, a canoeing instructor who works for Nigel and whose whole life is the sport; when things got bad, Nigel and Aled could watch out for Dad and me, while JW should be able to look after himself.

Early in our training we had to decide on which types of boat to use. Owing to our poor performance off Handa, Nigel thought we should paddle Aleut Sea II double kayaks. Although they had never been used on a major expedition before, these were much more stable than single kayaks, as well as being a lot faster through the water, so we should be safer. Unfortunately, Dad and I were never very keen on this idea: somehow it's not quite the same paddling a double. It almost seems like cheating. We were determined to get round Cape Horn in singles.

Now we knew we would have to work much harder. Nigel is a devotee of the Nordkapp; his battered old red round-Britain craft still rode the waves every time we paddled together. But while the graceful Nordkapps seemed to suit both JW and me, Dad never looked or felt comfortable in one. He said he felt too stiff. His fifty-three years, and the removal of a disc from the base of his spine, prevented his hips from swinging automatically as the kayak rode the waves. So Dad spent a lot of time developing his lungs, while waiting upside down for a rescuing kayak to help right himself. He tried various craft with a little more beam than the Nordkapp, doing most of his training in the Orion, before eventually finding the Ice Floe the most suitable, with its extra width and steering skeg. The eventual fleet comprised four Nordkapps, one Ice Floe and two Aleut Sea IIs. This was because our team had continued to grow.

Experience told us it would be useful to have along someone who could interpret not only language but also situation. No one fitted this bill better than Igor who was immediately keen. Canoe training would be a problem, but years of surfing mighty Pacific rollers in pursuit of the golden Peruvian girls who lay so plentifully along the beaches of Lima, had honed Igor's natural balance and athleticism. We decided he could paddle the reserve double, with Mark Hopking, one of our young instructors, controlling direction from the rear.

When John Boyce, the ITN cameraman, was added just a few months before the off, we realised that, if he were to use a hand-held camera, he would need a good strong man behind him in his double canoe. Chris Unsworth, Nigel's young and boisterous nephew, was chosen for this task; a cheerful powerhouse, Chris responded instinctively to Boycie's uncontrollable joie de vivre. Now we had a maximum nine people on the water at any one time: five singles and two doubles.

We had Admiralty Chart 1373 blue-tacked up in the pine-lined office at the end of the house for months, and I found it impossible to pass it without pausing to gaze at our proposed route. What would it really be like? We planned to launch the kayaks at the foot of one of the steep glaciers running down from Mount Darwin, at 2133m the highest peak in the Cordillera Darwin. We had hoped to follow the southern Chilean shores of the Beagle Channel, portaging all the kayaks and kit over a neck of land into Seno Ponsonby. This offered a much shorter and more sheltered route to Cape Horn Island, but the Chilean Navy would not give permission. Ever wary of their Argentinian neighbours on the north side of the Beagle, Chile insisted the whole area south of Cape Horn Island was a Naval Prohibited Zone. This meant we would have to paddle on east along the southern shore of the Beagle Channel to the isolated Chilean naval base at Puerto Williams on Navarino Island, where torpedo boats scan the icy waters for any sign of Argentinian warships speeding out of Ushuia on the north side of the Channel. From the Naval base, we would make our way through much wider waters, right round the eastern end of Navarino Island to Punta Guan-aco, before having to paddle twenty-two completely unprotected miles across Bahia Nassau to the shelter of the Wollaston Islands. This would be like crossing the English Channel, but rather less hospitable.

In our warm croft house in Scotland, we looked at Dad's slides of the three-mile-wide channel between the southern Wollastons and Cape Horn Island so many times: if he turned the projector off I could still see it on the screen. In my mind I was there, waiting for the weather window, looking across at Cape Horn Island with its 1400-foot cliffs and few landing places, waiting for the weather again to attempt the circumnavigation. All I had to do was be there on the day.

The most worrying time for me was the last couple of months before the off. I can now see why only five per cent or less of all trips ever get off the ground, and the more people involved the more complicated it becomes. Attracting sponsorship, planning, getting special travel permits, making sure you have enough of the right equipment and food, all take their toll. It is quite usual to be exhausted and run down by the time you leave for the trip, after all the hard training that has gone into getting superfit. We were no exception.

I was dogged by a succession of bad colds from late September 1991 until reaching the surprising warmth of southern Chile just before the New Year. I took every possible vitamin pill I could think of until Christmas. I wondered if this was a return to the sickly child I had been for most of my school years, or was it due to being tired after the season, to the continual douses of cold saltwater or just a result of pure worry? One thing was for sure, I would not survive the expedition if I was ill. I had had pneumonia before and knew that Cape Horn was not the place to get it again, so I kept gobbling the vitamin C, garlic pearls and cod-liver oil.

Dad and I also had to make great strides in our paddling skills during the autumn, if we were really to be able to survive the thirty-foot swell and giant clapotis that Frank Goodman talks of in his 1977 Cape Horn Expedition Report. Clapotis are pointy waves formed under cliffs where incoming waves collide with waves bouncing back, making the rhythm of the sea very irregular and disturbed, tossing your kayak in all directions. As usual, my imagination ran riot.

I had a recurring bad dream of becoming separated from the rest of the group, being blown sideways, knowing that I could not turn the nose of my kayak back into the increasing wind; the others would not see me because of the mounting swell, I could do nothing, the land was getting further away, visibility rapidly decreasing. Becoming more frightened, I would begin to panic, adrenalin rushing around my veins, heart thumping, paddle stabbing at the turbulent water. Soon I would capsize, the shock of the freezing water would put paid to any thoughts I had about rolling back up again. I knew there were only a few minutes in which I could sustain life. First, I would have to fire my emergency flares in quick succession before I lost feeling in my hands, then I would try to roll my body into the shape it had been in in my mother's womb to conserve heat, while holding on to my kayak. Drowning is supposed to be a "nice" way to die, but I did not fancy it much. Maybe I could drift away to a watery end, like my watery beginning.

I had great faith in Nigel and Aled's rescuing skills, but I knew full well that when the weather got to a certain point, there would be nothing they could do, we would all have to "paddle our own canoes", as the expression goes, and this extreme weather was what Cape Horn was famous for.

People who came to Ardmore on the adventure courses often ask what we are off to do in the winter. "You can't run an adventure school, without leading an adventurous life," Dad says. But this latest choice of "winter break" aroused strong reactions. "You're mad," or "You're very brave," were the usual comments, to which I would reply, "We'll have to see how it goes." What was I really letting myself in for?

The main spur to me, was that most people thought I would not be able to do it. I was not strong enough, and I did not have the skill required. Of course, I had great self-doubts, but I was determined to prove to myself and others that I could do anything in the expedition line where, in the end, it comes down to determination and not making mistakes. After all, I had had twenty-four years of training from my father, who believes in self-reliance. Mum and I had frequently been left to get on with things ourselves, and regularly given huge challenges to face.

We were due to leave from Heathrow on 29 December. But first there was a large family Christmas at Elsrickle, near Edinburgh, so we left Ardmore on 23 December.

I felt excited and unsettled. We were all in a bit of a state after days of weighing each item, packing and repacking to make sure we were inside the weight limit for our flight. I had wrapped some of my presents, but the rest would have to do in newspaper. The winter morning was dark and breezy. I said goodbye to my croft house aloud. I always do when going away. Number 76 Ardmore would always be my home, no matter where I was. I had spent my childhood in this house, and now for just over a year, it had been Justin's and my home. I wondered what would happen to me in the next months? Would I be the same person when I returned? Surely I would change? If something awful went wrong, I might not return. So much of life is, and should be, chance. By the time I returned there should be brave bulbs pushing through the dark muddy patch below the window, even snowdrops and daffodils out.

I walked down the hill gingerly, being careful not to fall on the treacherously slippery grass. As I turned to look at my other home, I could see Isso standing by the window, rummaging through one of her many bags. She had obviously been told to cut her luggage down. How different her life now was. The first six years of hunger and fear had changed into six years of love and a bounty of anything anyone could want. She was now strong, healthy and very much loved.

I was sorry Mum would not be coming with us on the trip, but while Isso was away at school, she wanted to be at home. It would be relatively peaceful and she was used to long periods of time alone. She enjoyed the solitude and was looking forward to getting some writing done.

Justin had already brought the fish farm's green aluminium assault craft in on to the beach and I dashed across to the smoke room to collect the freshly killed salmon we were taking down for Christmas. I quickly slit its belly open with a sharp knife to remove the guts, no point in carrying extra weight. The feel of cold running water on my blooded hands reminded me strongly of the winters I had spent helping Mum with the salmon-smoking, the desperate cold, and the smell of fish engrained our working clothes. They were happy times. The team of three, led by chief smoker, Mum, aided by me in charge of slicing and Ada, the greatest perfectionist ever, arranging and packing sliced pound packs, large sliced sides and trimmings for pâté before they were vacuum-packed and sent off as Christmas presents.

We said goodbye to Jenny and Alex, who had come to Ardmore in the summer to take over the job of maintenance engineer. Alex had also proved to be an excellent PT teacher, putting us through our paces during the last two months to make us supple. Hoppy and Dad took it all extremely seriously, which sent me into paroxysms of giggles. This was seen in a dim light, and I had to face the wall while doing my

Dad and Malc pause for breath below a high pass in Sendero Luminoso (Shining Path) country.

With old Don Pancho, Elizabeth's great uncle, on our quest for his missing nephew, Olaf Berg.

Very cautiously crossing an unfinished bridge on the new route we'd cut through the jungle.

Dad finishes off the wounded jaguar as it bites the pole.

Simeon and Roberto display their prize, but we were saddened at the death of such a beautiful creature, held sacred by the Incas.

Butterflies benefiting from the salt we sweated in our search for Olaf.

We caught up with Olaf Berg at last; Dad and Igor are questioning him about the murder of Elvin by the terrorists at Osambre.

Juan Huaman, Leocadia and Josephina inspect the packets of seeds I brought from Scotland. In the background are the forests of Choquesafra where the terrorists hide.

Raoul Beingolea, Dad and Igor planning the route.

The curious children who clustered round our camp reminded me so often of my sister, Elizabeth.

Elizabeth's mother, Leocadia, helping prepare supper.

Carefully getting out of the kayaks after a long day: nobody wanted to capsize amongst the ice.

◀ *Launching the kayaks from Compass Rose just off the Beagle Channel at the start of our 200-mile journey to Cape Horn.*

Hauling out for the night, then we'd have to find a level place for the tents and start cooking.

Paddling cautiously past a glacier in Brazo Noroeste on Day One and sixteen days later, heading for the rough stuff off the north-west corner of Cape Horn Island, still two hours short of the Cape itself.

exercises in order to control myself! We were already fairly strong for paddling, as we did a couple of hours each lunchtime. But being more supple would help us avoid capsizes and enable us to sit for long periods of time in the kayaks without becoming too numb and stiff. The exercises for the fish farm boys were too extreme for me. As it was, I discovered my hamstrings for the first time, having done quite a lot of running, which tightens them. Alex's leg stretches were agony. His final words to us were, "Don't forget to do your stretching exercises, and you'll be fine," as we sped off across the dark wind-ruffled sea loch in the boat.

I can never leave without looking back at Ardmore until its gentle green arm surrounded by rock-studded hills disappears out of sight behind a'Chadh-Fi Island.

In the usual scramble at the Green Point, while Justin held the bouncing boat close to the rocks with the mooring rope, a gust caught one of Dad's waterproof bags and bowled it down into the sea. As the female Ridgways held tight on to theirs, we watched him clamber down to the water's edge to retrieve it. This was not a good start to a long journey with the four of us cramped together in the car! I was glad the bag had not been mine. At least there was no repetition of the year before, when Dad and I argued so much that he threw all the coat hangers at me, like a knife-thrower at the circus, only he aimed to hit.

By the time we reached Inverness, the rain was pouring down. Would it be like this at Cape Horn? Probably far worse, according to accounts I had read by Eric Shipton. On we sped towards Elsrickle, listening at Isso's insistence to Carly Simon singing "Incy wincy spider" over and over again. Dad sang in a rather out-of-tune voice and decided this should be our song for the expedition because of the grit and determination the spider shows which leads to triumph in the end.

Christmas brings out either the best, the worst or illness in Dad. This time it was a mixture of the best and illness. He had a terrible cold which Isso had brought home from school. I thought I was getting it too, but did not say so. It was the last thing we both needed to set off for Cape Horn. My grandmother, her four children and all their children had made it for Christmas. There were seventeen of us in all. I had been looking forward to seeing all my family, but felt strangely distanced from the whole occasion. I knew that my grandmother was greatly troubled by me going away on another dangerous trip. She had always tried to talk me out of this sort of thing, but knew there was little point, as once my mind was made up, that was it. For the last year and a half, my thoughts had been trained on the canoeing trip. I imagined that a chapter of my life would close once it was over, and another would open. Now I just wanted to get on out there and do it, before something went wrong.

Dad and I flew from Edinburgh to London on Boxing Day afternoon to do last-minute things. He really enjoys packing and repacking, making lots of detailed lists and spending hours laying everything out; I hate it, so left my kit as it was, had a blood test, as one of the team had suggested that we should all know our blood group in case we ended up in hospital, and enjoyed some time with Justin who had flown down from Inverness for the last couple of days we would spend together for some time.

The Cape Horn team all made the check-in at Heathrow with plenty of time to spare. Nigel Tedeschi was the British Telecom research engineer who was coming with us to test their newly developed System C satellite communication, together with the Global Positioning System which would give us our exact position in seconds. He looked nervously at his huge trolley of spanking-new silver boxes plastered with BT expedition stickers, one of which crashed to the ground as the trolley was wheeled to the check-in desk. I could see Dad wince. How many more knocks would this sensitive equipment take before we saw it again in Punta Arenas? And how would Nigel manage it on a rolling sea while feeling cold and sick on the support boat?

Jack Tolson, the freelance camera man working for Survival Anglia, had an equally large trolley. His metal boxes looked somewhat more used than the BT ones, as he had filmed on expeditions before and had spent time with the British Antarctic Survey, so was quite used to transporting large amounts of valuable equipment half way round the world.

Nigel Dennis had already checked in. He knew better than any of us what he would really need, and was not one for carrying a lot of extra kit. He did not seem to feel the cold, and was still wearing his leather sandals. He had travelled backwards and forwards to Africa as a child, so was used to long hauls.

For Aled Williams they were something new. He looked frail, alert and a little nervous, in his purple ultra-fleece team gear, but I knew that once he was in his kayak, he could perform pure magic.

JW was furiously repacking, as he had just received some more gear from Nigel. He planned to stay in South America for a couple of months after the trip and, typically, was going to be prepared for every eventuality. Any weight over the allowed twenty kilos was extremely expensive. Luckily, the VARIG lady knew we were all off on an expedition, so overlooked the odd five kilos here and there, to our great relief.

The rest of the team who were flying out the next day had come to see us off, along with various friends and relations. I just felt blank, and hoped I would not cry when I said goodbye to Justin. I did not think the tough chaps would think much of that. At last we were allowed on the plane. One of the stewards asked me what I was doing with the two huge spoons I carried, referring to the split paddles. I smiled and said I was going on holiday and thought I might need them!

14

Punta Arenas

Dawn came with an apricot light over Rio, where we changed planes for San Paulo, the commercial capital of Brazil. Huge clusters of skyscrapers grew from the land like pins in a pin cushion that was spreading daily into the surrounding jungle. I was pleased to see jungle again, if even from a distance. At San Paulo we changed planes again and tacked west for Santiago, capital of Chile, where we made our final connection to Punta Arenas.

As we climbed out of the smoggy bowl in which Santiago is situated, the cloud cleared to reveal what could easily have been English countryside, green fields lined with tall trees, the only difference being that the backdrop was not the Cotswold Hills, but huge volcanoes, which from time to time erupt. The prevailing winds ensure that it is Argentinian sheep that suffer from these emissions: another way to get at your old enemy.

At the base of the volcanoes large blue lakes sprawl for miles, some dotted with salmon cages close to the edge. We landed at Puerto Mont, a wealthy farming area dominated by Germans, then took off on the final leg of the long journey to Punta Arenas. The great Pan American Highway ends not far south of Puerto Mont, and the wilderness begins. No one lives in this area. We saw the occasional road coming in from Argentina, maybe leading to the odd mine, but there looked to be nothing else, except more and more mountains, snow fields and massive glaciers. The plane followed the coast south towards Tierra del Fuego, land of fire and the end of the earth.

The first view of the Magellan Straits sent a shiver down my spine. I could see huge kelp beds just off shore. Ancient seamen were terrified of the kelp, believing it would drown them in its 150-metres-long tendrils. We were not sure how it would affect us, it must deaden the swell, but what if we were to become entangled?

At the tiny airport, which reminded me of Inverness, we were met by a smartly dressed young man who introduced himself as Second Lieutenant Eduardo Gahona. He was a Chilean marine officer, assigned to look after us and make sure we did not get into any trouble, or cause any. The Chilean authorities were no doubt concerned that with two cameramen in our team we were about to do another exposé on their country's appalling human rights record, or spy on their naval installations in the Cape Horn area. It was surprising, really, they had let us in at all.

Then Igor arrived in a flurry. It was great to see him again. I rather admire his seemingly carefree existence; at twenty-eight he still does not seem to work more than he has to and has no commitments. I decided that he was Dad's "long-lost son"! They get on well, as different as chalk and cheese, and find each other intensely annoying at times, but have great laughs together – Dad's cares seemed to fall away with Igor's exuberance. He looked much more serious than when I last saw him. Now he had short hair and glasses, but he was still his bubbly self with quick smiling eyes. Igor had spent Christmas in Punta Arenas, getting things sorted out, before we all arrived, and had booked us all in at the modest Residencia Roca, close to the port.

Dad and I shared a small room for two, while the other six slept in one big room. The plan was that when the final four arrived the next day, we would move into our tents to get used to them before the off. This had been Jack's idea. Obviously for a cameraman a tented team had more visual appeal than one enjoying the luxury of B & B. I thought it was a good idea, too, though I dreaded the prospect of mud and damp clothes, for from Dad's description I imagined the weather to be like Ardmore in winter: cold, windy and very wet.

Savouring the last of civilisation, I leant out of the tall shuttered window which faced the sea. Below, a bronze bust of Williams, a Welsh sea hero, stood alone on the edge of a once smart small plaza, but the surrounding buildings were now covered in graffiti. A naval barracks stood between me and the sea, the cadets alerted at various times of the day by a hand bell and orders over a loud speaker. There did not seem to be much action. I could make out some figures through an open window, but I think they were playing pool, rather than masterminding a grand military assault. Over the red corrugated-iron roofs of the barracks, the Magellan Straits rippled gently, a pale grey-blue reflected from the evening sky. Many large black and white birds squawked at each other, flopping off the rotting piers into the sea. These were cormorants, but with our initial excitement there was great discussion the next day as to whether they were penguins or not!

I stared out across the Straits, breathing deeply to soak myself in the evening atmosphere. It did not look so bad, there was no howling gale and no black rainclouds yet. I turned my head upwards to see a mass of cooing pigeons in the fine architecture above the window, busily sorting through their plumage, and squatting down for the night. I decided to do the same.

Dad was already awake when I woke at 5.30 the next morning. His snoring during the night had been so loud as to wake me; it was going to be an exhausting two months. Now he scratched his head and sighed, the familiar sounds that mean he is deep in thought and getting psyched up for the problems of the day.

We had to get the crate containing the kayaks, food and equipment out of Customs. As it was 31 December, everything closed at twelve noon, and goodness knows how many days' holiday there would be to recover from the New Year celebrations. Without the crate, we could do nothing. *Compass Rose*, the fifty-foot Dutch-built steel ketch we were chartering as our support vessel, was due to arrive at Punta Arenas in the next few days. We must be organised and ready to go by then.

So after breakfast Igor, Dad and I set off with the relevant forms on a round of Punta Arenas's maritime bureaucracy, acquiring and shedding clerks and conflicting instructions en route. We also had a letter we brandished when the going got sticky, from a Chilean Navy admiral promising to do everything to aid us in our mission, but it was 11.30 before we were at last reunited with our precious crate.

There were messages of good luck chalked on the side from the container-loading men we had met at Liverpool. It looked to be in one piece after its journey via Valparaiso, the only hitch having been that the ship carrying it from Valparaiso to Punta Arenas had "caught fire" and the cargo had come south by road! I could see no charred wood. The only damage was where the forks of a forklift truck had gone through one end. Luckily these had only punctured some of the dehydrated food, the two double kayaks were undamaged.

By now it had begun to rain. Igor hired a flat bed-lorry to take the crate to the marine barracks where Lieut. Eduardo Gahona had arranged for us to unload and sort out our gear. Dad and I hopped in the front with the driver, the others rode along side the twenty-three-foot-long crate to steady it. We persuaded the driver, who obviously wanted to get off at midday like everyone else, to go slowly, as the crate had to go back to Britain at the end of the trip. Dad's broken Spanish was not brilliant at this early point, but his sign language was always effective!

Once all the kit was unloaded, we pulled the crate off the back of the lorry on to a boat trailer which sagged alarmingly under the weight. It could rest here until our return. The rain had now become heavy, the prospect of sleeping in the tents was not a bright one. Lieut. Eduardo turned up in his uniform and we asked if we could sleep in the boat shed, but he frowned and said it was not possible. Perhaps it was a bit soon in our relationship to ask such favours. No one wanted to sleep in the tents, they all said they would prefer to pay for another night inside. Although Dad was not looking forward to the tent in poor weather, I knew he was cross and disappointed at everyone's decision.

Nigel Tedeschi set up his gear to check it was working after the journey. No doubt the marines were rather concerned that he was sending information about the lay-out of their barracks back to Britain, or someone else! But he managed to talk his way through what could have been a difficult situation.

We all trailed up to the main barracks past the huge cylindrical fuel tank, painted in disruptive pattern, through long wet grass with buttercups, and past some married quarters. The rest of the afternoon was spent in discussion. The job of dividing up the rations had been given to JW, as he is meticulous and would spend time doing it properly. The question he wanted to know the answer to was how many days should we plan for? This aroused great discussion in the team.

The air tickets for the main team were originally booked for a 20 February return, giving us plenty of time for filming and lost days through bad weather. Jack, Nigel T, Aled and Nigel had brought their return flights forward to 8 February, feeling confident that we could do the trip in thirty days, allowing ten of those days for bad weather. This was the first Dad had heard of this plan, and he was worried that the stronger kayakists would push on too fast at the beginning, causing my wrist to give out, after which I could paddle in a double if I was lucky or would have to go on the support boat for the rest of the trip, making the whole thing unnewsworthy as far as *News at Ten* would be concerned, as there was no first being achieved, and Survival Anglia would be let down too.

I could see Nigel's view that we should push on during good weather, in case of days stuck on shore, but I was very worried about my left wrist, which I had been resting for the main part of December. Would it survive many days of high mileage? It might not be me who got injured, but I felt everyone thought it would be me.

The discussion turned into an argument. Whenever there was a quiet moment, JW would ask, "So how many days should I plan for?" which would start the whole thing up again! I agreed with most of what Dad said. As ever, he was battling against all the others, but he has a certain unreasonable way of putting things across sometimes, which is just asking for a poor response. I know the feeling from years of discussions/rows with him! He knows exactly how to make people angry and upset, and uses this to the full. It usually gets results in the end, as his team try hard to match up to his high expectations, just to show him! But this new team did not know him as I did. All they knew was that the rumours they had heard about how difficult he could be were proving true.

The meeting broke up in a poor way. I feared there would be a lot more like this because there were too many chiefs and not enough indians in this party. Dad was the undisputed leader, he had planned the expedition for two years, recced the area and been to Chile on another expedition. He had thirty years' experience organising and leading expeditions, but he was one of the least experienced kayakists and worried about his fitness. Being twenty years older than the rest of the kayaking team, I wondered how he would get on with the others over the weeks. At least there was one person about to join us who would be on his wavelength. Richard Morris Adams, of similar age and a great friend, would understand him. Richard was coming along as co-ordinator, based on the support yacht. He was a terrific enthusiast and loved the excitement of the whole project. Between Richard and me we could surely keep Dad calm!

The inevitable irritations of making a film on top of completing the expedition were worrying to us all, but particularly Dad, who had been involved with films on several other trips and had particularly sour memories of the film made of the Whitbread Race in 1977–8.

Human drama is what people are interested in, and conflicts in a team are what make the drama. Jack had to make his film, but if he only did so when we all got on and nothing dramatic happened, the film would be boring.

Nigel was a natural leader, and had been running his own school of sea kayaking, windsurfing, multi-activity holidays and team-building courses for some years. His style of leadership was very different from Dad's. His was not the Army way, but he was effective. I could see problems arising between them. Nigel needed this trip to be a success, he also needed a change from the past few years which had been hectic and hard, building a new centre and keeping it going at such a difficult financial time.

Then there was Boycie, the wild ITN cameraman. There was plenty of scope for disagreement between him and Jack and there had already been some sharp words between him and Dad. The rest of us just muddled into the background, though I felt there was a lot of pressure riding on me.

Our main problem was having to wait for *Compass Rose*. A bunch of keen, fit young men sitting around with not much to do is not a recipe for harmony. We had all had enough of that over Christmas and now everyone wanted to get on out there and do it. But the Chilean Navy had insisted we have a support boat for safety reasons, and the cameramen also needed a firm base from which to operate. We had drawn up ground rules for this and agreed that it would be out of bounds to the five main canoeists except in direst emergency.

After the meeting the others went off to the duty-free shopping area outside the town with Eduardo. But I had made a list of a few final domestic items we needed for our tent, like a saucepan, an enamel mug and a couple of teaspoons to eat everything with. Shopping was never one of Dad's strong points, but I dragged him along.

We then kissed the famous toe of the bronze Patagonian which is meant to bring you good luck and bring you safely back to Punta Arenas. Patagonia means Land of the Big Foot, as the original Patagonian Indians, now extinct, had very large feet. The statue's big toe is bright and polished after years of travellers touching and kissing it. Dad kissed the toe on both his previous visits to Punta Arenas, and here he was back again. So there must be something in it!

We saw the new year in with Igor at the home of Hugh and Cathie MacLeay who Dad knew from 1970 and many recent phone calls setting up the support boat. Hugh was a sheep farmer but he had also built a hut in the Patron Hills in the section of Antarctica claimed by Chile and he let it be used as a base for the small but significantly increasing Antarctic tourist industry.

As midnight struck, car horns and ships' sirens blasted, fireworks and flares were let off, filling the sky with flashes of jewel-like colours. We stood outside in the warm darkness gazing into the sky, so different from our northern New Year's Eve. I thought back to the seeing-in of 1991. We had had fourteen for a three-day party at Ardmore, a great contrast to the usual mid-winter quiet. They were all friends who had worked at Ardmore in recent years. Then as New Year broke I had wept at the news that an old crofter friend on the Isle of Lewis had died and at the toast that was made to the Cape Horn team. "Where will they be this time next year?" were the words that were uttered. I was frightened. The weather was appalling, wet and windy. A fish-cage beam had broken, causing some drama, but was salvaged before we lost any of the contents. Now I was on the edge of my dream.

We had agreed to meet Lieut. Eduardo at the barracks at 10 a.m. on New Year's Day. He would open up the boat shed for us, so we could begin sorting out our gear and pack our kayaks. JW, Dad and I shared a taxi out there with all our kit. Dad was already in a bad mood as no one else had showed up for breakfast at 8 a.m. He felt that today nothing would be achieved after the excesses of the night before, and was this the way to be preparing to go into such a dangerous sea area? Surely we should be focusing on the task ahead.

The rest of the team arrived just after 10 a.m. JW and Nigel T began the job of dividing up the food I had been in charge of acquiring during the summer. From experience, we had decided it was best to have just two choices of main meal. If there were more you were always left with the least popular menu at the end of the trip, when things might be really critical. As we used Batchelors foods for expedition rations on the courses, we settled on their curry and mince and persuaded Brooke Bond, who own Batchelors, that they would like to provide it. With this great step forward, I then only had to find sponsors to give us breakfast, lunch and snacks. The numbers I had worked on were fifty-six days' food for nine people. Faced with the food mountain this had translated into, JW began by putting into four piles enough food for five days' paddling. The four piles were for the four tents. Hoppy and Igor were to share one tent and a double kayak. They were officially reserves, but would paddle whenever the weather was good enough and Nigel was happy to have them on the water. JW and Aled would share another two-man tent, but paddle their own single Nordkapp kayaks. Nigel, Chris and Boycie would share the only three-man tent. Boycie, being a vegetarian, was bringing his own special veggie evening meals. Nigel would be paddling a single, while Chris and Boycie paddled a double, Chris as the power behind Boycie when he wanted to film. Dad and I would share the last two-man tent, so that we could argue with each other and I could do the cooking!

Dad has never willingly cooked and lives on All-Bran, toast and sardines if Mum is away. On the non-stop round-the-world sailing trip he did with Andy Briggs in 1983, he perfected boil-in-the-bag curry on "a perfect bed of rice" and on his return insisted on giving Mum and me a demonstration complete with Camping Gaz stove and saucepan delicately balanced in preference to our electric cooker which might have been too big a test of his new skill.

While JW tackled the food, Jack filmed Nigel advising Dad which kit he would need to paddle in, and which should go in the kayak. Dad always liked the filming and cheered up a bit before heading off to the airport with Igor to meet the last four members of the team.

JW had oceans of personal kit carefully laid out on plastic on the dusty concrete floor of the boat shed, at least three times as much as would fit into his kayak and probably twice as much as any of the rest of us! He was always prepared for every eventuality, and special pieces of kit for special jobs were his hobby. He liked making gadgets and adapting old gear to new purposes. Though JW was a loner and wanted to be different from others, he was also an enthusiastic teacher and he would always notice if you were feeling down and help if he could. He had first come to work at Ardmore between school and university and grown a defensive beard to make himself look older when instructing people a lot older than himself. It remained, short and neat. His great interest in wildlife had turned to flowers as, with rather poor eyesight, he could never see the birds flying overhead well enough to identify. I remember him best from a minor drama involving a bucket of tadpoles while I was still at school. He needed a bucket and threw away what looked to him like muddy water. He was so contrite when Mum told him what he had done to my tadpoles, that he went and caught some more for me from a muddy lochan.

Packing a kayak is a finely judged activity. If you ram too much into a waterproof stuff sack it becomes too stiff to bend in through a hatch. After wrestling for half an hour with my sleeping-bag I wondered if every day was going to be like this, and gave up the struggle with relief when the final members of the team arrived from the airport. It was good to see them and to feel at last that the whole expedition could now come together.

Hoppy was bright and cheerful. I wondered how he would get on sharing a tent and kayak with the flamboyant Igor. Chris, a gentle giant with great strength, looked as if he was suffering from a night out with Boycie, though it could have been jetlag. Boycie immediately became the centre of attention by producing a special fibreglass casing to be fitted into the deck in front of his cockpit to hold his waterproof Sony Video 8 camera, when he was not filming. Aled thought he would be able to do it without too much bother. He was also going to drill two holes through the side of my seat for a back rest to be held in place. I had not used a back rest in training, thinking that without one, it would make my stomach, back and legs stronger. Whether this was true, I am not sure! No pain, no gain and all that!

I was glad to see Richard Morris Adams at last as I was going to need another supporter for Dad. I wrote in my diary:

I don't feel thrilled or special to be the only female in this team of twelve. I don't mind it, but don't feel really part of it, as I feel very loyal to Dad and have to try to make him keep calm and not get bad tempered with the others. Mum is much better at dealing with this than I am.

It was time for some lunch and Richard was borne off with the others to catch up on their news and no doubt be quizzed by them on how to deal with Dad, who had hauled me off to a different café. Later Richard explained what he saw as the problem: the team did not understand Dad's confrontational style, and kept wondering what they had done wrong. Why did it need to be a constant battle? Richard tried to explain to them that, in a strange way, Dad enjoyed and needed the conflict to get himself and everyone else going. He expected a hundred and ten per cent from his team, and took it personally if things were not going to plan or better. Richard could not change Dad's personality.

Next day Dad ran at 4.30 a.m. He was psyching himself up for the team meeting that was fixed for 11.00 a.m. Woe betide anyone who was late. But it was Dad who was held up, or was this a double bluff? Everyone else was at the boat shed and getting on with chores. This should please him, at least.

Hoppy was in charge of applying sponsors' stickers to decks and hulls: BT, Rockwater, RFS, Rolex, Blue Peter, John Ridgway Adventure School, Anglesey Sea and Surf Centre, they looked really smart, like a racing car. I just hoped my paddling would not let the image down!

With the worry of my wrist, Nigel advised me to use the Lendl split paddles I had brought out with me. The smart green and white Laser paddles we had been given by Wild Water were just a bit heavier, the shaft aluminium, so cold in the ice, the blades a bit larger than my rather battered red Lendl ones and the whole paddle a couple of inches longer. We could set the splits at a seventy-degree angle for a left-handed paddler, which would mean my left wrist would not need to bend as much as with the ninety-degree blades I had been training with. The possible slight loss in power should not make much difference at the speed we would be going. I was pleased to do anything to make it easier! This was one of the best pieces of advice I received on the whole trip, and was probably to make the difference between success and failure for me.

The briefing was set up outside in the sun. It was to introduce everyone to the filming and go through the responsibilities of our various expedition roles. Jack moved around amongst us with a camera on his shoulder. The controversial discussion that was held next was really the one that should have been filmed, but Jack had to be involved in it so, luckily, it was not! Dad writes in his diary, "Acrimonious discussion on finances, Nigel D walked out and Unsworth and Igor – so then I did." It had been my idea to talk about the money and how we weren't making a profit out of the expedition to help clear the air, but it had not worked. Maybe I should keep future bright ideas to myself!

At last, Saturday 4 January came. We had now been in Punta Arenas four full days, but this was the day we were going to leave. Because of the amount of kit, food and kayaks we had, we were advised it would be easier to get the necessary permits and Customs forms if *Compass Rose* sailed from Port Famine, sixty kilometres down the coast, rather than the large port of Punta Arenas, where they might be more strict and take longer. It seemed like good advice.

The road followed the coast, gently shelving stony beaches bordered by kelp beds, and broken occasionally by small rivers. We passed through a sparse settlement with low ramshackle wooden houses. How they survived the storms I cannot guess. But the rheas, that Dad had talked of, similar to ostriches, which in 1972 ran wild across the countryside, seemed to have disappeared.

The convoy climbed into a wooded area, still close to the coast, where Eduardo, who had come with us, called both vehicles to a halt. A large white needle of rock stood upright at a fork in the road. It showed the coastline of Chile, right down to its segment of Antarctica. This spot was midway between Chilean North and Antarctic South. Like Hugh MacLeay's hut, it was further evidence of how far Chile feels itself to be involved with the great icy land mass to the south.

Over a deeply rutted road, and down through a beautiful wood, we arrived at Port Famine, a small wooded bay, lined on one side by simple wooden bungalows on stilts, holiday cottages for marine personnel and their families. The four hundred Spaniards brought here to colonise the area by Sarmiento de Gomboa in 1584, had all died of famine and disease, maybe from eating shellfish affected by the red tide, which can kill in as little as three minutes. Eduardo told us of one of his friends, a fit young officer, who ate mussels a few weeks previously, lost his mind in twelve hours and stayed alive but delirious for three days until he died of muscle spasms. We felt suitably warned.

Richard, Igor and I went off with the lorry driver to the nearest settlement to see if we could buy some meat to barbecue for supper. The driver was really helpful, making sure we were not charged over the odds for a side of lamb from a small round woman in one of the only two makeshift stores, called, to Richard's delight, Provisions Richards.

The rain eased. Dad and I put up our tent, while Chris and Igor got the barbecue going in between Frisbee-throwing. Igor was in chaos. His large square bag on wheels did not work so well in the mud as in airports! Hoppy and he chatted as they erected their tent for the first time together. Nigel, Chris and Boycie already had their tent up, after a hunt for their pegs.

Eduardo went back to the marine base, after wishing us luck. He was to fly to Puerto Williams in a few days, where he would join us after our first leg. From Puerto Williams to Cape Horn, he would travel on *Compass Rose*, making sure that we did not stray into prohibited naval areas and telling us where the minefields were that had been put down to stop Argentinian invasion. Most of these were supposed to have been removed, but there seemed to be a little confusion as to exactly where they were!

Jack did his final Anglia interviews with the five main paddlers, walking on the grass just above the crescent-shaped beach, littered with dead kelp. I talked of my fears, mainly my wrist, and how excited I was on the eve of getting going.

We had a jolly evening, eating delicious barbecued lamb, bread and soup. Richard began his first watercolour. I had the last shower for a long while before turning in. Dad was already in our tent, muttering about his new tin-opener which had broken at lunchtime. Nigel's Thermos flask had also broken. From now on the kit must stand up to the rigours of the journey, or we would have to do without. *Compass Rose* should arrive during the night, we would set off tomorrow morning.

15

Towards the Ice

Dad woke us all early next morning with the news that *Compass Rose* had arrived. I had slept well, maybe I was getting used to his snoring, or maybe I was just exhausted. I put a pan of porridge on for our breakfast, then rushed up to the ancient cemetery on the hill overlooking the bay to get my first view of our support boat. She looked good and seaworthy, her white hull catching the early morning sun. I thought of those sixteenth-century settlers who must have waved farewell to the vessel that landed them here with such hope and fear in their hearts, only to end up in this graveyard.

Compass Rose's skipper, Conrado, was a bushy-haired bear of a man with large stomach and a soft voice. He agreed to risk the kelp and bring his boat into our bay for loading, so our team sprang into action, making a human chain, the way we move everything at Ardmore. On board, Richard our quartermaster together with neat JW stowed away all our rations. Two trips out in the inflatable saw everything on board, except for the metal boxes of BT and film equipment, which we decided to slip on board after all the various officials had made their inspections, to save any meddling with the contents or risk of confiscation.

A harbour official turned up to check *Compass Rose*'s radio communications were working. Two Navy officials arrived in the afternoon to check the safety equipment. Then the Customs man came and checked us all off against our names, luckily not wanting to see our passports which were now well buried. By the time he was off, and we could leave too, the wind had changed direction and begun to get up, *Compass Rose* swung dangerously into the thick kelp close to the rocks. The Magellan Straits had turned from being a millpond to a mass of white horses in just a few minutes, and I had not even taken my seasick pills!

We hurried the metal boxes aboard and then paddled out the kayaks.

The wind gusted, cats' paws shot across the cold dark grey surface. I thought how embarrassing it would be if I capsized on the way out to *Compass Rose*, but luckily it did not happen!

All on board, the heavy anchor was lifted, covered in huge long strands of kelp, and we headed out into the Magellan Straits. We were all excited and stayed on deck until evening chill drove us below, all except Igor who didn't want to risk being seasick so stayed shivering behind the dog house with the crew's fresh meat, a naked lamb, hanging from the end of the mizzen boom.

We passed the infamous Isla Dawson where hundreds of political prisoners had been held during Communist rule. It looked bleak, there would be little chance of escape, and to what? Conrado told us of the bounty of freshwater fish in this area, he had taken five Chileans on a fishing trip to Isla Dawson the year before on *Compass Rose*, and they caught forty-five large trout on one day. Dad's eyes lit up, he would love to be on a fishing trip.

The wheelhouse of *Compass Rose* was a completely different atmosphere to *English Rose VI*, where those not on watch sleep and those on watch are on deck. On *Compass Rose* we were not sailing. Conrado was very much in charge, but the mood was typically South American and relaxed, with loud music in a warm area where six or seven people could sit as well as the helmsman. Lucho was the engineer, drove the inflatable and was in charge of taking the thick stern line to the shore for secure mooring. He was small, nimble, strong, married and the same age as me. Pato, the cook, had been a diver before joining *Compass Rose*. He whipped up delicious meals for the fifteen of us in those first few days, and was always laughing and joking. Slightly older than Lucho, he had had a couple of disastrous marriages, and was accident prone, but a great asset.

We anchored for a late evening meal in a beautiful steep-sided wooded bay with a river flowing down from the mountains. It was called Beaubasson. I almost expected a square rigger to sail through the bay entrance or a group of Feugan Indians to emerge from the trees and stare at us with wild eyes. It was so completely untouched and beautiful.

Things were rather cramped for the first night. We had four bunks, two slept round the table, three on the false floor between the bunks, one in the wheelhouse and Chris and Nigel on deck. But we all slept soundly as the crew raised the anchor shortly after 1 a.m. and headed on south, towards the glaciers below Cordillera Darwin. The cold waters were filled with phosphorescence. It seemed that at every turn there were new and wondrous things not to miss in this seemingly barren land.

I woke after 7.30 a.m. Up in the wheelhouse, Conrado was consuming his breakfast of *yerba mate*, a revolting local drink, like strong spinach mixed with old fag ends. Boiling water is poured on to the chopped-up dried herbs to form a thick mixture in an avocado-shaped gourd, then with a special silver straw with a strainer at the bottom, the foul-tasting liquid can be sucked up in small sips. One sip was enough for me.

The day was filled with stunning views and squalls from the north-west. The thick treelife began to thin, and we had our first sight of snow-covered mountains and glaciers in the distance. The land became more barren, with ice-scraped rockfaces, cold ruffled seas, and sea lions leaping with joy, while albatrosses with their plank-shaped wings glided effortlessly on air currents all alone. The coastline was similar to north-west Scotland, I felt very much at home.

We passed Isla Basket, named after the basket-shaped boat that the crew of Darwin's *Beagle* built when the Indians stole their boats. Fuega Basket was the name they gave to the only girl among the four young Fuegan Indians Darwin brought back to England.

Towards the end of the afternoon, we saw our first penguins, and some of us took those ridiculous photographs which, when developed, show a tiny dot of a bird in the far distance! We should reach the glacier where our kayaks would be launched by the evening. Conrado decided to anchor for the night on the southern shore of Brazo Noroeste at Caleta Voilier. This should be a sheltered anchorage, free of ice, from where we could set off early the next morning across to the north side of Brazo Noroeste and into the treacherous ice-filled waters below Mount Darwin.

By the time we reached Caleta Voilier, it was after 9.30 p.m. and beginning to get dark. Conrado switched on the echo sounder and kept checking the chart, to get over a shallow sill of rock at the entrance to the bay. The echo sounder beeped loud and alarmingly, as the water got shallower. The engine raced to slow us down, we crossed safely, but only just. Once in the bay, however, Conrado found that it was not safe enough to anchor, with a narrow beach hemming the steep sides, dropping away to deep dark water. He carefully took *Compass Rose* over the sill again, echo sounder beeping and engine racing. The light was nearly gone now, there seemed no suitable places to tie the stern line ashore to, the water either too deep or too shallow. Eventually, Conrado and Lucho decided just to drop seventy metres of chain. They would sleep with one eye open, and if the wind changed we would move.

This problem confirmed Dad's fears that the support boat would nearly always be in more danger than we would. We could always pull our kayaks out of the water if the weather changed, but *Compass Rose* might have to go miles to find a suitable sheltered anchorage.

Conrado was not at ease, and not pleased. He looked at me and said, "I have anxiety in my stomach." Then retired to bed.

I woke just before 6 a.m., from a dream of digging my small garden at home, spreading rotten seaweed on to the rich dark soil. But the seaweed was long and heavy and seemed to have a will of its own, the giant kelp featuring in my subconscious.

When the anchor was lifted we headed out into choppy Brazo Noroeste. Waves broke over the boat, putting paid to JW's ever on-going repacking. I changed into my Helly Hansen Super Lifa thermal long-sleeved top and bottoms, Wild Water dry bottoms, spray deck and dry cagoule, wellies, thermal headband to keep my ears warm, sunglasses and cap against the glare, topped off with my buoyancy aid, which was now loaded with all sorts of emergency kit and felt more like a bullet-proof vest.

The yacht was filled with excitement, noise and chaos. I think Richard, Jack and Nigel T were looking forward to the nine kayakists getting off so that they could gain some order.

Directly north, across Brazo Noroeste from Caleta Voilier, we motored into more sheltered waters. Soon the sea turned a milky turquoise with the melt water from huge glaciers deeper in the fjords. Taking the right fork towards the Romanche glacier, we were suddenly confronted by huge walls of fissured ice, compacted and contorted over thousands of years. Lumps of ice floated all around us, and Lucho stood on the bow pointing out these small icebergs, as Conrado motored slowly ahead, with echo sounder on. We tucked into a bay with steep cliffs down one side and a rocky beach on the other. Conrado was pleased with this as an anchorage, but would not risk going any closer to the dangerous pack-ice that lay at the base of the glacier and ran out into the channel for a mile or so. After the anchor had been set, Lucho whizzed ashore with stern line and secured it to a strong-looking tree, as we danced around the deck, stuffing the last few items into any hatch they would fit, before lifting the kayaks over the side and on to the inflatable, where JW and I carefully lowered them into the water and tied their bows together. Soon all five singles formed a red and yellow fan on the flat turquoise-green water. I was dying to get into my boat, to feel the difference of paddling with it fully laden, to get used to the new angle of my paddle blades, and to go among the ice as close to the groaning and crashing glacier as we dared, for it had already bewitched us.

The two 23-foot double kayaks were carefully lifted down on to the inflatable, heavy when empty, extremely heavy when fully loaded. Then I slid carefully into my yellow craft – foot rest felt fine, back rest good and spray deck on securely. The kayak was a lot deeper in the water, and because of the weight, slower to get moving and slower to stop. It did feel a lot more stable being so heavy, but then rolling might be harder. I would have to remember to keep it slow. One by one, the others slithered into their boats and we set off towards the ice. The sky was blue and clear, while the sun shone bright and strongly. It felt so good to be paddling again.

With my first few strokes towards the ice, I thought of Messner's advice to Brian Blessed before he set out to attempt Everest. Messner told him that the first step must always be linked with the last. This would remain in my mind for the whole trip, and probably my life. If I could stick to this, apart from unforeseen problems, I should succeed.

I could have watched the giant glacier for hours, with its deep blue fissures, and dirty hard-packed snow that was now ice after thousands of years' compression. Periodic thundering crashes heralded another few tons breaking away and falling hundreds of feet into the sea below, causing tidal waves in which the pieces of pack-ice bumped together. To our amazement, there seemed to be a family of ducks living at the base of this glacier, though what they lived on and how they survived the constant barrage of falling ice-blocks I could not make out. How close could we go? JW came up with the theory of twice the distance from the base as the height of the glacier itself.

Jack filmed from the inflatable and from the shore, as we carefully picked our way through the ice. Boycie filmed from the front of his kayak, picking up the crunching sound of the ice and the enormity of the glacier in front of us.

We had to paddle round huge lumps of ice, like small sculpted islands, before we put ashore at a small ice- and rock-strewn beach. It was now late afternoon, the sun was setting, shedding a more gentle light on our harsh surroundings. We must pitch our tents soon, and get into the camping routine. The simple way of life suits me well, I like to make the best of the few possessions I have with me, and enjoy getting the cooker going, discovering fresh water, laying out my bedding, cooking supper and eating in the open air with such a fantastic view.

We lifted our kayaks high out of the water, Dad and I tied ours together with his tow line and to a tree, remembering the freak high tide that flooded his and Mum's tent on his previous trip to Patagonia. If this happened here, we would not want to lose the kayaks!

Everyone was in very good humour as we made our separate ways across the mossy carpet under small trees to find a good campsite. Dad and I put our tent up together, then put our supper of dehydrated mince into water to soak. The cooker worked like a dream and I had supper cooked in just a few minutes. The mince, peas and mashed potato tasted really good. I knew the others would complain about our limited diet to start with, but people will never admit that something like mince is good. Dad and I made a deal: if I cooked every night he would do the washing up. I quite enjoy the cooking, doing the best I can with the small amount of raw ingredients, but do not like feeling that Dad is not doing his share, so washing up and putting up the tent seemed a pretty fair deal, because I would have to help with the tent anyway!

There was some evening toing and froing from *Compass Rose* and Boycie, Chris and Nigel returned from a photographic foray. I feel very selfish in places of great beauty and quiet. I want to enjoy them on my own in silence, without others distracting my concentration from the whole engulfing wonder. I feel this often at Ardmore. Experiencing the mountains or the wood with others is not as intense as doing so alone. Maybe this is why I love the cinema so much. For the length of the film you are totally taken up by what you see and feel, with no interruptions.

With a pan of warm water, I retreated into a gully in the slabs of scarred rock leading down to the ice-filled sea to have a wash. What a glorious view there was from my bathroom window! I washed my underwear and hung it on a tree in the vain hope that it would be dry by the morning. On the way I discovered a heathery plant with small white bell-shaped flowers and some giant white daisies. I wish I had been able to collect these strange plants, but my kayak was full enough already without pressing flowers!

The Nordkapp HM

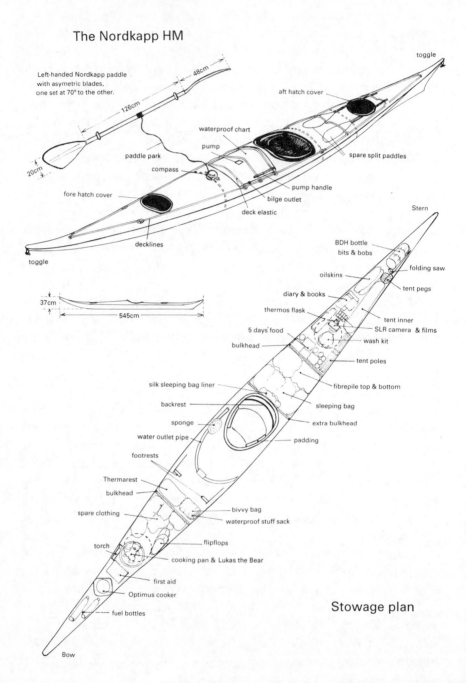

Left-handed Nordkapp paddle
with asymetric blades,
one set at 70° to the other.

48cm

126cm

20cm

paddle park

compass

fore hatch cover

waterproof chart

pump

toggle

aft hatch cover

spare split paddles

pump handle

bilge outlet

deck elastic

decklines

toggle

37cm

545cm

Stern

BDH bottle

bits & bobs

oilskins

folding saw

tent pegs

diary & books

thermos flask

5 days' food

bulkhead

tent inner

SLR camera & films

wash kit

tent poles

silk sleeping bag liner

fibrepile top & bottom

backrest

sleeping bag

sponge

extra bulkhead

water outlet pipe

padding

footrests

Thermarest

bulkhead

spare clothing

bivvy bag

waterproof stuff sack

torch

flipflops

cooking pan & Lukas the Bear

first aid

Optimus cooker

fuel bottles

Bow

Stowage plan

With my scarf tied round my head, I could still just smell the remains of Christmas perfume in this cold and barren land, as I settled with a mug of cocoa, my bare feet in flip-flops, camera poised to catch a huge icefall, while writing my diary for an amazing first day. The months of hard work and doubt and training that had got us to this point seemed to fall into place. It had all been worth it just for this one day.

Dad always woke first, but we needed the extra time as we were the slowest to get organised. I remembered Nigel saying at one of the training sessions in Anglesey, "I can be packed, have eaten and be paddling within half an hour of waking up!" It was true, but he had had a lot more practice than we had, and did not have so much kit. Dad was usually stiff in the morning, helping him into his kayak and getting his spray deck sealed around the cockpit properly was part of my job as tent mate. I did get a little short tempered at times!

Boycie was raring to go, with his camera poised, so with Chris in the double, JW and Nigel in their singles, they set off to the base of the glacier to see if they could capture on film a huge lump of ice falling and the tidal-wave effect on the kayaks. They went as close as they

> ▶ Sleeping kit, clothes, food, Thermarest were completely sealed in Ortlieb and Wild Water waterproof stuff sacks, the rest in plastic bags.
>
> ▶ JR and RR shared their camping kit. In his kayak JR carried: tent flysheet, extra groundsheet, half the food and water bag (on deck).
>
> ▶ I wore while kayaking:
> > thermal headband, waterproof camera round neck
> > Supa Lifa thermal top
> > Wild Water canoe cagoule with latex neck and wrist seals and double neoprene waist seal
> > Wild Water Expedition buoyancy aid
> > Supa Lifa thermal long johns
> > Wild Water dry trousers with neoprene fold-down waist and latex ankle seals
> > double seal spraydeck with neoprene body and shoulder bracestow line around waist cotton socks, wellies
>
> ▶ My Wild Water Expedition buoyancy aid with reflective tape for night paddling contained:
>
> in small top pockets –
> > sun screen block 15, total sun block for lips and nose, lip salve, fudge bars, plastic whistle, hand compass, air temperature gauge, spare film
>
> in larger lower pockets –
> > Therma balaclava, sou'wester, sun glasses, pogies (gloves that Velcro over paddle shaft), 8 mini flares, diver's knife
>
> in large back pocket –
> > survival suit

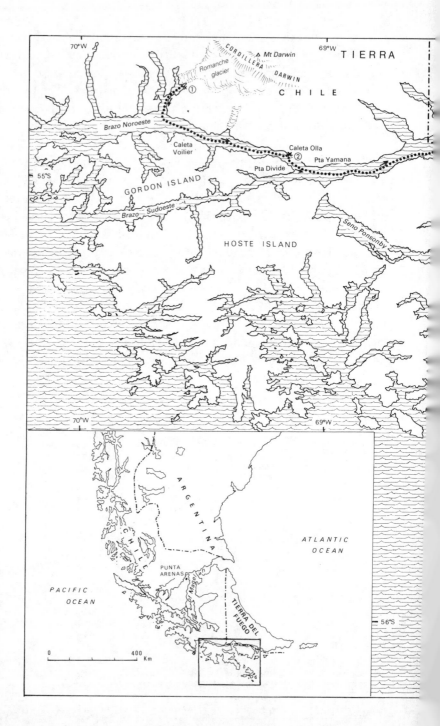

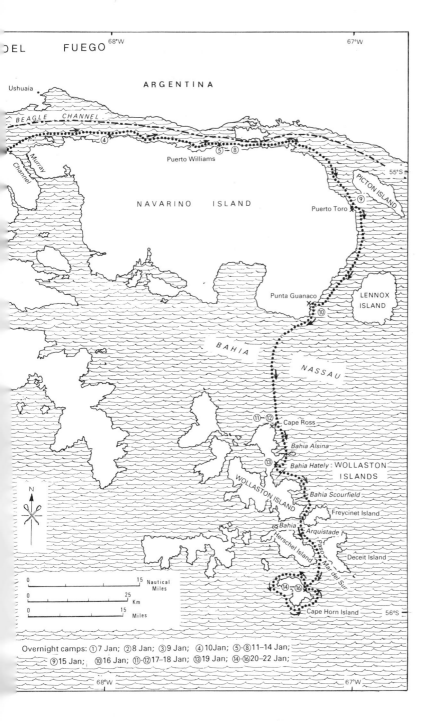

DEL FUEGO 68°W 67°W

ARGENTINA

Ushuaia

BEAGLE CHANNEL

Murray Channel

④

⑤-⑧

Puerto Williams

55°S

NAVARINO ISLAND

PICTON ISLAND

⑨

Puerto Toro

Punta Guanaco

LENNOX ISLAND

⑩

BAHIA

NASSAU

⑪-⑫ Cape Ross

Bahia Alsina

⑬ Bahia Hately : WOLLASTON

ISLANDS

WOLLASTON ISLAND

Bahia Scourfield

Freycinet Island

N

Bahia

Arquistade

Herschel Island

Paso Mar del Sur

Deceit Island

0   15 Nautical
               Miles
0   25
                    Km
0   15
              Miles

⑭-⑯

Cape Horn Island   56°S

68°W   67°W

Overnight camps: ①7 Jan; ②8 Jan; ③9 Jan; ④10Jan; ⑤-⑧11–14 Jan;
   ⑨15 Jan;   ⑩16 Jan; ⑪-⑫17–18 Jan; ⑬19 Jan; ⑭-⑯20–22 Jan;

153

dared, and began shouting, leaving us more pathetic kayakists struggling to get into our boats without tipping ourselves into the icy water. We paddled away from the glacier towards the open water, knowing that they would catch up. On hearing particularly loud cracking gunshot and thundering sounds we turned to see the biggest chunk yet falling into the water. At that distance the kayaks below looked like tiny bright dots trapped in the ice.

They caught us up, still high on the adrenalin of the encounter and laughing at Boycie who had warned them not to swear if anything dramatic happened, because they would not be able to use the sound track. But when the tidal wave hit them it was Boycie's "Oh, shit!" that went on the tape.

Compass Rose caught us up as we headed out towards Brazo Noroeste. The early morning was perfect and calm. The sun shone brightly down on us, the ripples left by our paddles and the wakes from our elegant kayaks sparkled as they caught the light. Once away from the ice, the steep sides to the fjord again became covered with trees. Large black and white Savage ducks waddled along the rocks on the shore, our passage not quite frightening enough to make them take flight. This is one of the bonuses of kayak travel. They did not look very "savage" to me. The large white males reminded me of the pair of white ducks I had given Mum for Christmas as a surprise present a few years earlier. Carrying two huge ducks in along the track to Ardmore on a windy, dark December evening had not been easy, but well worth the surprise it gave her on Christmas morning when she opened Lance and Ada's hen house.

JW and I chatted away, as Dad paddled ahead with Nigel. I was very conscious of my wrist, remembering Messner's words of wisdom. I could feel slight twinges but could not decide if these were real or in the mind. JW, who always had the odd pain here and there said that his wrists were a little sore too. After five miles, we came into the large open channel of Brazo Noroeste and stuck close to the northern shore. The day was hot. I steamed in my dry suit, thinking the weather more suitable for a day on the beach; not what I had expected at all.

Jack asked us all to paddle close to *Compass Rose* so that he could film us, while Pato became wild with enthusiasm as he threw carrots and apples to us! Maybe the last fresh fruit and vegetables we would get. I was amazed at the support, generosity of spirit and excitement from the crew, they really seemed thrilled to be involved in such a venture and looked forward to the unknown waters of the Beagle Channel ahead.

We had been warned that the ozone layer was reported to be very thin over southern Chile at certain critical times of the year when the angle of the sun was low. Sheep and salmon were apparently going blind, people were getting skin cancer and not letting their children play outside at certain times of day. Boycie was to do a story on it for *News at Ten*. None of us knew how seriously to take this scare but it was noticeable that we all plastered ourselves with our various strengths of barrier cream.

Dad had daubed white sun block all over his face, and wore his father's old fold-up sunglasses which completely covered his eyes and were held round his head by elastic, making him look like some sort of giant bluebottle. JW was also very careful, sleeves pulled down to the wrists, and with a leather nose-protector on the sunglasses turning him into something like the Elephant Man. Igor favoured brightly coloured zinc warpaint, trendy purple-tinted sunglasses and cap; his kayak partner, Hoppy, had the cap and glasses with blobs of white sun cream that had not been rubbed in properly over this face. Aled had put on his skiing goggles and plenty of sun screen, also his floppy sun- and sea-spray shield, which he had made from neoprene. A Fuegan Indian would have found us quite alarming, though our paddling technique might not have measured up.

We came to a huge hanging glacier with thousands of gallons of melt water pouring out in a violent waterfall down the ice-smooth rock to the milky sea below. One lonely iceberg floated out into the main channel. Thousands of feet above, the glacier looked most precarious. This was the southernmost exit of the Romanche snow field. The glacier was much cleaner and bluer here than at the end where we had spent the previous night.

The building, but as yet, gentle breeze changed direction several times, mostly from behind, the west, helping us on our way, but sometimes it began to head us. At least it was cooling.

We stopped for lunch after paddling sixteen miles in a wide and very shallow gravelly bay, with thick trees all around and a glacier further inland. I had a lot of water in my cockpit, and hoped Aled could find the leak. But a bigger worry was Nigel who had mentioned a painful lump on his wrist earlier in the day. Dad thought it was probably linked to a small infected cut on his thumb. Now he mentioned his wrist again, which meant he must be in a lot of pain, as he would never do so normally. Deciding it must be tino synovitis, he paddled out to *Compass Rose* to get a wrist splint. It was not a good sign for day one.

As the afternoon continued, the wind got up, and Brazo Noroeste became quite choppy with white horses. I stuck close to Dad, who always says he thinks he is about to go in, but does not! I could feel my kayak beginning to dance again, as in the months of winter training. The secret to keeping upright is all in how relaxed you feel and being able to move with the kayak rather than fight it. It was good to feel the boat dancing again.

The huge, smart, white *Ocean Princess*, belonging to Lindblad, steamed past us towards Ushuaia. They called us up on the radio, and wished us the best of luck. Picturing those wealthy tourists sipping their gin and tonics while looking out of the portholes at us gliding through the waves towards our goal of Cape Horn, I felt really proud to be where I was. I wouldn't have changed places.

Nigel fell behind over the last mile or so. The sea became more choppy with small pieces of floating ice. We were all fairly tired, but Nigel must have been in agony. Aled and I brought up the rear of the group, with just Nigel behind us as we turned into the sheltered waters of Caleta Olla. Hemmed by a short yellow gravelly beach, tall trees crowded the rest of the land. Two large brown birds of prey sat high up on the trees watching us with interest.

On reaching the shore, after more than thirty miles, my legs felt weak and stiff from sitting down for so long. My shoulders were weary too, but my wrist had held out and I was pleased with the day's paddling. I had proved that I could do it.

Nigel sat next to his kayak on the beach, quiet, head down, arm raised, while his team put up their tent. Here was the first drama for Jack to capture on film, he interviewed Nigel and Dad separately. Neither were thrilled with what had happened, Dad is not one for handing out a lot of sympathy.

Rushing to get our tent up before the rain, one of the poles snapped. Dad and I squabbled about whose fault it was as heavy drops started to fall. JW had read the instructions on how to mend the tent poles and helped with it, so our tent went up in the end. Dad dived in and I made for the shelter of thick trees to do the cooking, wearing my huge yellow oilskin smock and flip-flops.

Igor dashed around following Conrado's instructions on how to make a Sargasso poultice for Nigel's wrist. This was an ancient Indian remedy for strained muscles and tendons, using long strips of seaweed which set like a plaster cast around the damaged limb when dried out. During supper, the rain stopped and the sky cleared to reveal a beautiful if chilly evening. JW came to our tent and said he thought that Nigel was in shock. This was strange, tendonitis would not put someone into a state of shock. Maybe there was something else wrong with him. Poor Nigel. Everyone thought it would be me who would fall by the wayside. He was the last person any of us expected to go sick. He must have been feeling terrible about that, as well as in pain. I looked in on him later but he was asleep, so best left undisturbed. I also caught Dad getting Igor to wash up for him in the sea, and gave him a rocket!

Boycie and Chris had lit a fire on the beach and, as with all camp fires, we were all attracted to it like moths. At last it died away and the evening light began to fade. Time for bed. I felt encouraged by the distance we had covered, but worried about my "shadow" on the water. Nigel was always there when you were close to your limits. Once more I climbed up the small bank to see if he had woken and needed anything, but he slept on soundly.

16

Beagle Channel

At the eastern end of Gordon Island where the Brazo Noroeste ends and the Sudoeste begins is Punta Divide. It's here that the infamous Beagle Channel starts. We reached there early next morning, minus Nigel who was running a temperature aboard *Compass Rose*. Perhaps we had not got the Sargasso poultice right.

After studying the chart so often during the planning stages, I had built up a picture in my mind's eye of what the Beagle Channel would be like, but as ever it was different. The sea calmed down and became relatively flat after the effects of wind and tide further back. The sun shone brightly again, after the rain of the night before, and JW and I rafted up to take off our cagoules. Then the wind changed direction and began to head us, making paddling slightly harder work and cooling us quickly.

We reached Punta Yamana, a small point in the middle of nowhere, with a house on it. This was a Chilean radio station. As Dad and I landed two huge dogs bounded down to the water's edge. When had they last been fed? Dad used his best sheepdog-scaring voice to stop them coming too close, while we perched on a precarious ledge to have some coffee and a bite to eat.

The dead kelp on the beach had gone pale and looked like bundles of intestines, among the odd plastic bottle. We soon climbed back into our boats and paddled round to meet the others. Dad pointed across the channel to the spot where we had originally hoped to portage all the kayaks and kit over into Seno Ponsonby, making our route to Cape Horn shorter and far less dangerous. We could have hugged the coast, and been in the lee of the land for the majority of the time. But the Chilean Navy had not let us go this way, due to naval installations in the area. This had conjured up all sorts of images of nuclear-weapons factories selling to Iraq, and huge warships, but having now seen the terrain, this was all highly unlikely! Anyway, the planned portage looked pretty steep to me, even from a couple of miles across the channel.

Nigel was up now, with his arm in a sling. He stood on the deck of *Compass Rose* looking grey faced. Surely someone with tendonitis could not look so ill as this? He recommended to us that we should cross the Beagle Channel to the southern shore now, rather than later. Fifteen miles ahead was the Argentine border on the northern shore, but the southern shore is all Chilean. It would not be a good idea for us to land in Argentina. We would have to cross today and, with the wind and tide against us at the moment, it would be best to cross at the narrowest point. Nigel and Aled thought we might get into slack water close to the southern shore, which would make our paddling easier. I was prepared to take any advice, for we now seemed to be leaderless on the water. Although Aled was a fantastic paddler, he had no ambitions in the leadership and communication stakes and was probably rather apprehensive of Dad, who now made all the water decisions, talking by radio to Nigel on *Compass Rose*. I think Aled felt that just paddling along was pretty boring. His interest in kayaking was all in the technical skills of paddling tide races and white water in his squirt boat. To me, the basic skills were all I needed to provide a wonderful means of travel that allowed me to see beautiful wildlife and scenery, as well as enjoy the water. Maybe if I was as proficient as Aled, the techniques in which he revelled would become more important to me, too.

We became quite separated while crossing the Beagle Channel. It was calm, but how long would we survive if one of the feared williwaws, famous for uprooting trees and throwing ships on their sides, came rushing down from the mountains? Dad and I stuck together, and most of the time close to Igor and Hoppy in *Rockwater 7*. Igor was always in buoyant mood, and ready for a laugh. He began to teach me "useful" Spanish phrases. "We must cross the channel," and, "Oh look, there is a sea lion," were the two for that morning. JW liked to be on his own, paddling some distance behind, absorbed in his own thoughts, but I did feel that he would be keeping an eye out for us. Boycie and Chris were well away with their Walkmans, Boycie just waiting for one of us to go in, or something dramatic to film.

The weather became cloudy, and we continued heading into the wind. It was nothing like as hard as most of the training we had been doing at Ardmore in the autumn, battling across Loch Laxford into hailstorms, our eyes stinging with the douses of cold saltwater. But the psychological feeling of wind and tide against us did not make it any easier, and now we were paddling all day, not just a few hours. My left wrist began to twinge and I went back to keeping my thumb on top of the shaft to give it a rest.

By the time we stopped for lunch, on the southern shore of the Beagle Channel, the rain had started to fall. The wind dropped and we sat on a pebbly beach under tall trees that grew right down to the waterline. A small stream ran down the middle of the beach, fresh water for us to refill our water bags which we kept under the deck lines of our kayaks. My bottom was wet, and so were my wellies. Aled had not managed to locate the leak and as the icy puddle in my cockpit got deeper it seeped in down the back of my legs. But after a tin of sardines and a few oatcakes, I would be ready to press on.

After lunch we paddled across a wide bay, Dad and I some distance in front of the others. We chatted most of the way and I felt that he was really beginning to enjoy himself.

What began as a tiny dot on the horizon turned into a large sinister grey ship. Dad thought it was a research vessel. It continued on its course up the centre of the channel and, when it came level with us, let off a couple of massive hoots from its horn. We felt so small, vulnerable, and worried about its great wash. Shivers ran down my spine as the noise took over everything for a few brief seconds.

Compass Rose caught up with us and Pato threw two oranges, which I stuffed down the front of my buoyancy aid. The others caught up in dribs and drabs, as the weather worsened and the sea condition became more choppy. We really must keep together now. I was worried about Dad, he could not afford to capsize and come out of his kayak in this freezing water. With the rougher water, our hands were wet all the time, and with the distances we were covering it was likely that blisters would develop.

Boycie and Jack both filmed as squalls whipped across the slate-grey water's surface. They were almost like vultures just waiting for the kill! I felt a little unsteady and did the odd wobble. I was sure Dad would be feeling uneasy, too.

Over the last five miles of the day, we were in touch with Nigel on *Compass Rose*. He still looked like death. In fact he looked worse each time we saw him, his eyes sinking deeper into his head. He had been trying to get through to the naval commander at Puerto Williams to ask once again if we could go through the Murray Channel instead of all the way round Navarino Island. He was going to play heavily on the fact that "the señorita was very tired" and also mention his own problem. Dad had no faith in playing the Latin gallantry card. But then gallantry is not part of his make-up. He had been trying in vain for over a year to get permission to go this way. Naval manoeuvres in the area, we were always told, were the reason we were turned down.

We stopped to have a break in the shelter of some small islands, and alarmed some Steamer ducks, strange birds who cannot fly, but seem to run across the surface of the water using their wings to help them get along, but never quite taking off.

The last few miles were becoming painful. We paddled in with aching muscles, among small wooded islands and I felt the first signs of chafing from my buoyancy aid under my arms. Jack and Richard went ashore ahead of us to film from above, and nearly got attacked by wild boar on the beach! I got out of my kayak and sank almost up to the top of my wellies in gluey, smelly mud. Not being able to pull one boot out, I fell hands forward into it, a great way to end an exhausting day! But the glorious campsite made up for any feeling of exhaustion. We had just covered over thirty miles in around ten hours, and now, fifty-five miles into our journey, had already achieved over a quarter of the distance in two days.

After supper, armed with shampoo, flannel and toothbrush, I made my way towards the nearby river to take a bath, while Dad took the pans to wash further upstream. I washed my hair first, dunking my head in the stream and using the saucepan to pour icy water over my head to rinse out the shampoo. It was skull-crushingly cold. But as my eyes slowly came back into focus, I saw a brown furry shape sitting on the opposite bank, some twenty feet away. It was a sort of beaver or platypus creature, and it munched away at its supper, quite undisturbed by the gasping and squawking noises I had been making. It was another of those moments that made the whole trip worthwhile.

Everyone was in high spirits that evening, eating their supper, laughing and joking, everyone except Nigel, who looked grey, tired and worn, though he still put on a brave face. He had his wrist bandaged, and held it up high on his chest with a tight sling. Dad looked at his arm.

Richard had mentioned that he had a red line making its way up the inside, and Nigel said he was still feverish. Dad knew what this meant, and had seen it before; it was almost definitely blood poisoning, and very serious. Once the red line reaches the heart you die.

We were all on the water at 7 a.m. next morning, except Boycie and Chris, who said they would catch us up. We paddled out through the islands we had so wearily paddled in past the night before, out into the Beagle Channel, where the wind was fresh, and cats' paws sprang across the water, clawing at our paddles. Leaving the peaceful Islas Campamenta behind us, we must cross the bay and entrance to the Murray Channel, before reaching the relatively safe coastline of Navarino Island.

It turned out to be a strange day, starting with white horses and north-westerly wind Force Four-ish, cold without my dry cagoule on. No sign of the other double for some time, until *Compass Rose* steamed up, with the double being towed on the Zodiac, Boycie below having been sick and Chris with suspected tino synovitis. Two more down! Boycie should recover fairly quickly, but what of Chris?

We tucked in behind an island after crossing the open bay, and rafted up next to *Compass Rose* to get the latest news of the sickies. Amongst those of us who were still on the water, there was quite a sense of camaraderie. We were the survivors who must keep the dream alive. It seemed to me like running a marathon: you can run all the way, or you can run most of the way and walk some, or you can drop out through injury or lack of training. I wanted to run all the way, slowly but surely, anything else would seem like cheating.

We had a short break on the island, drinking coffee, eating fudge and laughing with Igor. I collected some giant horse-mussel shells entwined in cocoons of seaweed on the beach, to take home with me, and put next to the conch shells from the Cape Verde Islands, collected on the winter sailing trip when I was seven and the giant fir cones from the redwoods in North America after running in the New York marathon fourteen years later.

The wind died away and sun reappeared with renewed vigour, turning the day into a real scorcher. We now feared sunstroke and heat exhaustion, which was crazy in such a generally cold, wet and miserable part of the world.

The tide was completely different from the day before. It seemed to be with us now, when the same time yesterday, it was against us. This lifted our spirits. We paddled on through small islands, any bare skin again covered in sun cream. JW had his fingers well taped, protecting his blisters, while I just had one on my left middle finger.

Pato dived off the side of *Compass Rose* into the still-icy sea, which shows how hot it was out of the water. None of our boat team, however, decided to join him!

Hugging the opposite shore, we now approached Argentine Ushuaia, the southernmost city in the world. Its name is Yahgan, and means Bay Penetrating Westward. Its landward side is surrounded by deep forest, and shelters under the Martial Mountains. Because of its geographical situation, everything has to be taken in and out by ship or plane. The deep bay and port can take large ships which bring in food, merchandise, petrol, cars and machinery, and take out wood, wool, skins, frozen meat and *centolla*, or king crabs, a delicacy from these southern waters. Eighty per cent of the 7,300 inhabitants are employed by official agencies such as the Navy, Forestry and National Parks, which means that they are only resident for a couple of years.

As we paddled along, looking across the Beagle Channel towards the sprawling city under its pall of dust or smoke, I tried to imagine what it had been like in 1870, when Thomas Bridges, an English clergyman, set up the first Anglican Mission here in Tierra del Fuego. With his wife, Mary, and their baby daughter, they became the first permanent white settlers. Their life must have been frightening and hard, surrounded by semi-savage Indians and reliant on growing their own food in the harsh climate. In 1872, they had a son, Thomas Despard Bridges, the first white child born in Tierra del Fuego. Another couple, the Lawrences, arrived in 1873. Six Bridges children and five Lawrences grew up speaking four languages: English, Spanish, Ona and Yahgan, the local Indian languages, which Reverend Bridges taught himself. He produced a Yahgan dictionary, and also translated parts of the Bible into Yahgan. The children grew up to follow in their parents' pioneering spirit. I could not help thinking that when it came to pioneering my own parents came from a similar determined mould.

The afternoon provided mixed weather, suddenly getting a lot rougher, so we stopped to put our dry tops and bottoms on, in case we went in! The wind and waves came from behind, pushing us on well, but we did not feel as fresh as we had done after two full days. When the wind died away again, I paddled close to a lone sea lion, which seemed to be sleeping, only splashing and diving away at the last minute.

Dad and I were the last to struggle through the kelp to our campsite that evening. My shoulders were tight and aching. We had covered nineteen miles, not bad, but not brilliant, another fifteen miles to Puerto Williams, the Chilean town and naval base on Navarino Island.

We heaved our kayaks up on to the grass, and while Dad walked up the slope to find a suitable flat spot for our tent, I stripped off my sweaty salt-marked dry top and bottoms, and wellies. The rocks felt sunkissed under my damp tired body. A warm gentle breeze lifted stray tendrils of hair, soothing my burning face. Physical exhaustion is a "luxury" that not many people ever feel in our mentally busy times, but so worthwhile – especially once you've stopped doing whatever was exhausting you!

Dad came back down the bank, telling of a beautiful flat patch of grass he had found dotted with sweet-smelling white clover. It would be like our croft in summertime, when the sheep are out on the hill to graze.

There was an Indian burial ground a little way round the bay. I had read a lot about the Indians of this area, and felt desperately sorry for them, wiped out, as usual, by the white man's greed and disease. At least these southern Indians died out after not too many years of change to their natural way of life, and were not turned into a pitiful travesty of themselves like their northern counterparts.

The day had been a victory for British Telecom. Richard came ashore to tell us Nigel T had sent a message from Nigel D to his home on Anglesey, listing his symptoms. Nigel's wife had telephoned the doctor and got the diagnosis and treatment. Within twenty minutes, the message came back that Nigel did indeed have blood poisoning and he must start taking antibiotics as soon as possible. They would fight the blood poisoning, but without getting to a doctor and more treatment, he could still die.

Dad was worried that the barometer readings, so crucial in judging the change in weather, were not being plotted properly each hour of the day and night. If there was a sudden drop, and it kept falling, strong winds were bound to come. After Richard had returned to *Compass Rose* in the Zodiac with Lucho, the wind suddenly began to build, the stove kept blowing out and in a matter of five minutes the Beagle Channel was white with sea spray, huge rollers surging forwards. This was one of the feared williwaws.

We checked our guys and weighted our tent with extra rocks, then I went down to the beach to watch *Compass Rose*, as Conrado manoeuvred her to safety after quite a battle. The crew, our boat team, Igor and the sickies were all on deck in their waterproofs, straining to lift the anchors which had both dragged. Sick or not, all nine hands were needed on deck, as the violent wind took hold of *Compass Rose* from one side then the other, throwing her this way and that. Over the noise of the wind, I sometimes caught the frenzied sound of her engines pushing forward.

I fear the wind, we are so helpless against its great force. Always having boats in the water, during winter gales at Ardmore, I have memories from early childhood of the wailing sound, the clanking of the rigging and the unease it casts over our small house, clinging precariously to our relatively sheltered hillside.

Once the anchors were out of the water, there was the problem of cutting away the great tangle of kelp which had become twisted around the anchors. This had to be removed, otherwise they might not go down the right way up, and would not set properly. The wind was not lessening any, and the men on the deck could only just stand up. Communications were almost impossible, except by sign language, and all those who could clip themselves on had done so. But small and nimble Lucho, dressed in an old coat and moccasins, hopped over the bow on to the anchor; hanging on with one hand, he cut away the kelp with the other. He really was a star in this sort of situation. Now all Conrado had to do was find a place where his anchors would hold!

As I peered into the almost complete white-out of the Beagle Channel, I could just make out a yacht with no sails, being pushed before the storm down the far side of the Channel. We were relatively calm and sheltered in our small bay, but the bare-poled yacht was completely at the storm's mercy, travelling faster than it would under sail or power. Would they make it into Puerto Williams? Or be swept out into the Atlantic? I was glad to be on shore. On *Compass Rose* meanwhile, it looked as if Conrado was edging back to safety and Lucho and Chris could take ropes to the shore. Out in the Beagle Channel the yacht had gone.

I sat down close to our two kayaks looking on in awe at the weather which had come up so quickly. I thought of my bad dreams of being separated from the others, or just not being able to continue physically. I knew I could not possibly survive such weather as this on the water. I doubted anyone could. This time we had been spared.

Lucho and Chris were heading towards me in the Zodiac bringing a thick rope. As they got close to the shore, Chris leapt over the side, up to his thighs in water, and dashed ashore with the rope. I heaved the bow of the Zodiac up on to the rocks, and held the boat for them while they tied the rope round the strongest-looking tree. Chris was in a great state of excitement, adrenalin coursing through his veins, but what about his wrist? He must be careful with it if he wanted to paddle again. I felt Dad's words in my mouth, but did not utter them: "Slow it down, keep calm and use the brain."

Once everything seemed to be under control, Nigel called up again from *Compass Rose*. He said that Conrado was happy with the setting of the anchors, but JW and Aled's kayaks looked a bit vulnerable, could we get a message to them to lift them up higher and tie them down?

We had got into the habit of camping separately because Dad pre-ferred a quiet end of the day to unwind and, though I sometimes missed the others when their laughter or the smell of their camp fire drifted along the shore, I could not deny I too enjoyed the solitude. Now I gladly trudged along to their end of the bay to deliver Nigel's message. Hoppy was already asleep in his tent, while Igor was still out carousing on *Compass Rose*, JW was preparing the supper while Aled slept. He seemed to have the greatest capacity for sleep of anyone I had met. All in all I was amazed at how unaffected they all seemed by the horrific gale that had blown up!

After planning an early night, I eventually got into my sleeping-bag at 9.15 p.m. Dad and I now slept head to toe, so that I could kick him more effectively when the snoring got too bad! Just as I was drifting off a gruff Spanish voice said, "Hello, hello," and started banging on the tent, and there was Lieut. Eduardo, and a couple of other chaps. He said that the weather had been so severe, he was worried we might have had an accident, so persuaded his friends to drive along the dirt track as far as they could in case they could see us. Eduardo was certainly relieved to find us safely ashore, and left us to go to see Conrado and discuss what should be done about Nigel. We would cover the fifteen miles to Puerto Williams tomorrow if the weather subsided.

As we approached Puerto Williams, with a brisk north-westerly pushing us on, we paddled below the airfield where one of the twice-weekly scheduled flights from Punta Arenas had crashed into the freezing sea a year earlier, drowning many of the passengers. It's true that you don't remember distant disasters, but hearing about this one on the news at home, one cold dark morning, I knew I could be there one day and now here we were.

Puerto Williams harbour was guarded by menacing grey and black warships which dwarfed and overshadowed the sprawl of low pastel-coloured wooden houses beyond. There was a cluster of yacht masts away to the right, but one yacht close to the warships caught our immediate attention, not because a diver seemed to be doing something to its hull, but because it was a Bowman 57-foot just like our own *English Rose VI*. How amazing to find one here, when only about nine were built.

We paddled on towards the cluster of yachts, and got out on the beach next to the "yacht club", a bar at an angle, housed in an old warship that sat on the bottom, filling and emptying with the tide. All round the walls and upstairs on the bridge were flags and messages from famous yachts that had visited.

Igor and I went to look at the *Sea Tomato*, a boat which had been rowed from Cape Horn to Antarctica. It was red and fairly small, but larger than *English Rose III* which Dad and Chay Blyth rowed across the Atlantic.

Nigel was whisked away to hospital by a naval doctor and Eduardo took the rest of us up through the town to one of the only two hostels, called Hostal Ona-ashaga, which means Ona's Channel, the Indian name for the Beagle Channel. Everything inside was hardboard – floors, walls, ceiling and doors. Mario, the landlord, was amazed and delighted by the number of us. We discovered later that there had been only sixty-seven guests in over a year.

After a cold shower and a sleep, we went out to see the small museum, with its many haunting photographs of the last of the Indians, maps of where the different tribes had lived, pictures of how they made their teepees from animal skins and foliage, and travelled in canoes with their fire always burning in the middle of the boat. It was the women who swam ashore to moor the canoes in the kelp and dive for shellfish. Not many of the men ever did swim. I hoped that none of our team got any ideas from this! There was a lot too about the dreaded white man, who brought religion and tried to make the Indians "civilised", but wiped them out. Half way up the stairs were photographs of Frank Goodman's team who paddled round Cape Horn in 1977, starting and ending their trip here. One of their wooden paddles hung on the wall. They all looked such big tough chaps. Could I really do it? Upstairs was a menagerie of dusty stuffed animals and birds. They all seemed so big – huge penguins, albatrosses with massive wingspans, sea lions and many others, including my friend the beaver, called *castor* in Spanish.

In the main square we met Jack and some of the others, who had just come from the hospital. Nigel had been admitted for several days. He was now on a glucose drip, taking the maximum dosage possible. The doctor said he was lucky to be alive, a few more hours and he probably would have died. This shook everyone, though when Dad started muttering about the expense of keeping *Compass Rose* idle a row almost broke out in the street. Dad clearly felt that blood poisoning was something which should have been avoided. Richard and I made a tactical withdrawal of Dad, to have afternoon tea. What a treat. Seated at the Formica table in an otherwise empty café, we guzzled our way through plates of toasted buns covered with butter and jam.

A middle-aged American couple came into the café, looking rather lost, and asked, "Do you know the ropes around here?" Roger Swanson, a pig farmer from Minnesota, proved to be the owner of *Cloud Nine*, the Bowman 57-foot we had seen in the harbour. He had read some of Dad's books, and even had one on board. They were soon getting on famously, discussing various things that they had added or changed to the original fittings. We would go and visit them later, as they were setting sail for Antarctica early the next morning.

Then Eduardo appeared, to shepherd us along to a meeting with the local naval commander. Commander Swett was very tall, distinguished, and spoke good English in a deliberate nasal voice. We sat down at a boardroom table, on our best behaviour and discussed the chart of the area from the Beagle Channel southward to Cape Horn, which filled a wall. It was slightly grubby after years of worried fingers tracing routes around the coastline. The seemingly more powerful Argentinians were always a threat, not least before and during the Falklands War, when Puerto Williams was not sure whether it was about to be attacked, or the Falklands.

Dad and the commander discussed the route we wanted to take from here to Cape Horn. Eduardo had been saying it was impossible for us to go the way we wanted, due to naval manoeuvres and nature reserves in the Wollaston Islands. Commander Swett recommended that we hug the coast of Navarino Island to Puerto Toro, a naval base some twenty-two miles down the coast. The wind should still be with us that far, but half way down the east coast of the island, it often blew from the south. The next day we could reach Punta Guanaco, an eighteen-mile paddle, with thick kelp close to the coast if the chart was correct, but I could not really believe the whole coastline would be kelpbound. At Punta Guanaco we would be positioned at the closest point to the Wollaston Islands to wait until the weather was right for our sea crossing, twenty-one miles, the same distance as Dover to Calais, and the most dangerous part of the whole trip. If the weather became bad, all we could do would be to turn and run with the wind, and it would be unlikely that that would be to the closest land. It was a huge commitment. The bad storm of the day before was still very fresh in everyone's mind. Wind speeds of 170 kilometres per hour had been recorded at Puerto Williams, and the pier had been partially wrecked. "The worst in living memory!"

We would aim for Cape Ross, where there was a Chilean radio station, and from there we must travel down the eastern side of the Wollaston Islands, past Bahia Hately and Bahia Scourfield, between Herschel Island and Deceit Island to Cape Horn. We had wanted to paddle in between the Wollaston Islands, with the possibility of exploring and seeing whales, but this was not allowed. Again our planned portage from the relatively sheltered Seno Alberto across to Bahia Hately would have to be abandoned.

Commander Swett traced the route with his index finger, and on arriving at Cape Horn Island itself found the door handle to an inner office had taken the place of most of the island! He turned the door handle, and like a South American Inspector Clouseau, peered inside the office, as if to find Cape Horn! It lightened the rather fraught atmosphere in which we had just faced up to the extent of our commitment.

Before we left we also discussed the hiring of the lone helicopter stationed at Puerto Williams, as Jack and Boycie both needed film of us off Cape Horn from the air. Because there was only one helicopter, it had to have a ship, called the *Castor*, positioned in the middle of Bahia Nassau in case it went down over the water. The ship took seven hours' steaming to get to its position, so we needed to give at least seven hours' notice before we wanted the helicopter. We hoped not to take more than six hours for our circumnavigation, so the timing of this whole operation was going to be crucial, as the weather could change so much in seven hours. With the ship costing nearly a thousand dollars a day, and the helicopter charge by the hour, there could be only one call-out. But it was important that this did not make us take chances we should not.

It was odd to see the whole team all together on dry land. In the café where we had eaten the toasted buns, tables were set up in a long line. At one end sat Conrado, and at the other sat Dad. I was next to Lucho and taught him and Pato various useful English words, like "fish and chips" – the only choice on the menu, which had been ordered in bulk in the afternoon. Richard supplied wine for us all, which helped the evening continue with great gusto, ending for some in the yacht club in the small hours.

The next three days while we waited for Nigel's recovery were difficult for the expedition. This is what tests team spirit. It is not the glamorous action parts which are the hardest, but the unexpected delays and in-activity when you are keyed to go. We learner kayakists had done all right so far, but we were only too aware of how much we should depend on the experience of the experts once we reached the open sea to the south of Navarino Island and headed for the Horn. But for now we had to kick our heels. The weather was chilly and wet, turning the dirty streets into a muddy quagmire. I at least had my piece to write for the *Weekend Telegraph*, which I then managed to wipe out, due to my lack of word-processor skill. This left me something to do for the next day! I am also quite good at sleeping for hours on end. But for those who needed the stimulation of action it was desperate.

We went to visit Nigel in hospital a couple of times a day. He was beginning to look a bit better, though his face was still drawn. Dad's heat rash was bad, and not helping his humour at all. Neither did the cortisone injection in his backside. His snoring was terrible, too, despite everything I threw at him in the night. I asked Mario if I could move to another room, but there wasn't one. So I eventually shared with Igor, who did not come in until around 3 a.m. and then slept like a baby.

Hoppy and I went for a run out of town along the coast to the east, hoping we could find a route back inland, and ended up clambering through the forest, hitting the road by a sign saying, "Keep Out, Military Zone." Sheepishly we ran back to the hostel, hoping no one had seen us!

The best thing about our enforced rest was having clean clothes, washed in a washing machine, smelling of soap, ironed and dry to put on. The longer we stayed here the harder it would be to get back to damp salty underwear. It was also a convenient time to sort out various technical problems with *Compass Rose*'s radio and generator, both essential to our media obligations.

Before we left, we visited the meteorological officer, who worked in a hut on the edge of the runway, surrounded by huge ledgers, large machines that periodically clunked and clicked to produce a typed message and up on the wall two dials which showed the wind speed and direction. He was horrified by our plans and, instead of giving us advice on how to tell when bad weather was about to strike, kept saying it was suicide and didn't we realise wind readings at Puerto Williams could generally be doubled for Cape Horn. I felt shaken and afraid when we left him, but not put off continuing. We were going into an area greatly feared by everyone who had anything to do with the sea, but it also has a magnetic attraction as a testing-ground for ultimate challenge. You get to be a bit of a sucker for that sort of thing if you grow up with my father.

17

Open Water

A few people off neighbouring boats came down to the shore to watch us set off early on 15 January. "Are you sure you know what you're doing?" someone asked.

Nigel was back on board *Compass Rose*, along with Eduardo who had now joined us fulltime. In theory he could summon the Chilean marines to our aid if there was a drama, though this seemed a bit farfetched, as by the time any assistance arrived it would surely be too late. I rather thought that Eduardo was with us to check on what sort of film we were really making, and not let us go into any of the restricted military zones. Whatever his function, he found watching us paddling along hour after hour boring and cold work and he muffled himself in his Antarctic gear and a large disruptive-pattern fur-lined hat with earflaps.

Our first day to Puerto Toro went well. Everyone was glad to be back on the water. Boycie was now fully recovered, and Chris strapped his bad wrist and used my left-handed paddle. He never complained. The scenery was becoming more beautiful as we got out of the Beagle Channel. We passed a couple of large ocean-going ships en route to Puerto Williams, and *Compass Rose* radioed them not to come too close with their huge wash. Dad and I were quite nervous as we had a good sea behind us anyway. There was now far more kelp close to the shore and we either paddled very close in or a couple of hundred yards off to keep out of it. We stopped for lunch at a beautiful bay among the bent and twisted southern beech trees that this area is famous for. They get smaller and smaller as you head further south. The last couple of hours of the day were tiring, into a gusty wind. Richard appeared from the galley hatch of *Compass Rose* with his chef's hat on and a tray of biscuits about to go in the oven! He was having such fun.

The rusty hulk of *Lobo I* still lay on the reef where she sank in a storm in 1988 off the north end of Picton Island. She was owned by the Mission Society and had been carrying a cargo of religious books, mainly bibles. What sort of a message from God had her fate been? We started to see flocks of Rockhopper penguins, which looked comical and awkward leaping through the water, but they came as light relief while paddling. Now the coastline became more steep and forested, with waterfalls dropping straight into the sea, and after a real struggle into the wind we reached Porto Toro where a sea lion sat high up on a rock at the bay's entrance. Porto Toro is now a marine base with only a few civilians and a small school. Over a hundred years ago there were three hundred gold-panners there, now there are only two somewhere down the coast.

As soon as *Compass Rose* moored at the good wooden pier, Richard hopped off with a box of rather brittle, but delicious, freshly baked ginger biscuits. He was good at keeping the troops happy and we were all in great humour, after a pretty tiring twenty-two miles. The officer in charge of the base offered us a huge new shed to sleep in, and hot showers. The water was almost black, even darker than the peaty water of Ardmore. A young soldier lit a fire for us in the middle of the concrete floor with damp wood which soon smoked half the team out, and a small puppy, who tried to drag our kit away as we were unpacking the kayaks, went on to attack Dad while Igor, Chris and I were interviewed by Nigel with Jack filming. The interview was, in consequence, a disaster as we failed to keep straight faces. It is not true that only girls giggle!

The *Castor* arrived as I was searching for our supper in my boat. The smart Chilean naval officers were fascinated by the kayaks, but put their trust in the *Castor*, reinforcing our belief that the sea crossing of Bahia Nassau could be far more dangerous than the actual circumnavigation of Cape Horn. I put this firmly out of my mind as I enjoyed the treat of getting into my sleeping-bag, clean from the shower and with a high possibility of having dry clothes to put on in the morning, as they steamed with everyone else's round the fire.

My alarm was set for 4.45 a.m. and I woke to hear Nigel and Dad talking about the weather. It was good. We must get going as soon as possible if we wanted to reach Punta Guanaco that day. I was up, packing my smoky kit away and off to the shower room. Another treat was an invitation to breakfast with the duty officer, who stuffed us with freshly baked bread rolls and butter, and huge mugs of steaming Milo. This was a great start to the day, better than more oatcakes and sardines.

Dad and I spent most of the morning paddling along close to Igor and Hoppy, being treated to tales of Igor's beach-bum way of life. He taught us to sing "*La Cocaracha*", about the cockroach who did not want to walk, because he had no marijuana to smoke! We also sang, "Boating Down the River", but rather badly.

During our lunch break, a breeze blew up and the sun disappeared behind sinister cloud formations as the lone figure of Nigel paddled towards us from *Compass Rose*. He felt his arm was healed enough to rejoin us on the water and the short afternoon would be a good test before the sea crossing to come. Dad went down on to the beach to meet him, and they discussed the worrying-looking weather, deciding that we should get straight back on the water, and paddle down the coast to Punta Guanaco as quickly as possible. Here we could hole up until the bad weather passed. The forecasts that Nigel had received on *Compass Rose* were for severe storms.

As we paddled along the coast, we could see and hear the building surf rising and falling on the steeply shelving beach that ran almost uninterrupted to Punta Guanaco in the hazy distance. The land was low and flat now, and would offer little protection from the wind, whichever direction it came from.

The team had quite a different and more purposeful feeling about it now that Nigel was back on the water. We moved faster, and closer together, with Nigel scanning the shore for possible landing places. There was more communication too. I felt happier, and I am sure Dad did.

The chosen landing spot was quite close to the point itself, but far enough away from it to avoid the larger surf. The beach was made up of large round boulders, and landing required luck or judgement. One way or the other, we all made it just as the rain began to come down in stair rods. The evening looked a little grim, with only a few stunted southern beech trees to shelter a campsite we might be at for some time. I was soon cold and wet, but ignored the discomfort, knowing that once supper was cooked and I was inside the tent it would all seem a lot better. The curry burnt and the rice was a little watery, but it was hot and nutritious and we were too hungry to notice the burnt bits. The wind and rain continued for most of our meal, but as we were finishing, the pitter-patter stopped and the tent became bright and sunlight flooded through the yellow inner tent.

We planned a 3 a.m. start, weather permitting, next day so, while Dad settled for an early night, I took my wet kit to dry by the fire the others had lit, and we sat round it enjoying what was now a calm, sunny evening.

We were all nervous about the sea crossing which would take at least five hours non-stop, during which time anything could happen with the weather. I am sure everyone had their own private fears, but there was great mirth around the fire, as Boycie started to singe his trousers while filming as we cried and gasped with the smoke! I got everything dry, including my wellies, and left them to their wine (which Igor always carried in his boat) and kedgeree.

Hearing Dad's snore, I picked up my camera and walked along the curving beach. The tide had fallen, exposing slippery green boulders. Flocks of small birds flitted across the waterline. How did they survive the violent weather of this area? A couple of Savage ducks waddled, slipping and sliding over the rocks, throwing themselves forward into the water to escape. I walked close to the bank, collecting shells and feathers. The cold wind blew in my ears under my scarf and the crunch of pebbles blotted out any other sounds until I stopped in my stride and heard a chewing noise. There was a large beaver sitting high on a tussock, chewing the bark off a stick. I moved towards it, it saw me, but kept on chewing. When I was about six feet away, the beaver stepped down from the tussock and waddled along a well-trodden path towards the waterway where it lived. I followed close behind, it did not seem concerned by my presence. Into the water it slid, and swam slowly, eyeing me up and down until deciding it had seen enough and diving into the muddy waterway, leaving only a trail of bubbles.

Returning to the beach, I looked across to the east at Isla Lennox, about five miles away. Would we be blown back on to it when we attempted the crossing? I was afraid. I felt fairly strong and at ease in my boat, my wrists were standing up to it well, but my real worry was the wind. I was not as strong as the men, and if we had to paddle for hours against a building wind, how long would I be able to keep going?

The alarm went at 2.45 a.m. I turned it off with my eyes closed. It was pitch dark outside. There was no sound of rain or wind. Dad called up

Compass Rose, and Jack told us the sea was calm. In his opinion we should go for it. Nigel came on and, after a brief conversation, we began to move, so as not to waste any of the good weather. Igor was in total disarray; not being an early riser, he was finding this one hard!

"There's one thing I hate, and that's sea crossings," Nigel muttered as he walked backwards and forwards urging everyone to hurry. I stuffed the shells from the night before into one of my hatches.

Launching from the rounded boulders was easier than landing, though there were still alarming scraping noises of fibreglass against rock, which caused me to feel pain. We had all paddled out into the cool silk water by 5 a.m. It was like a dark giant, calm and sleepy, but when it woke, what would it turn into?

My wrists twinged, but I decided this was just nerves. I felt excited inside and frightened too. Nigel said his wrist was okay, only a slight twinge from time to time, but he must have been nervous because if things started to go wrong, he and Aled would have to do their best to get us out of it.

We were soon off Punta Guanaco, where we encountered an oily cross-swell, the water changing direction rapidly. I felt comfortable, but could see Dad was not. He stuck close to *Rockwater 7* and I followed him. He had given instructions that if he and I both capsized I should be rescued first! He said that he had had a long life and I was too thin to survive long in the freezing water.

JW had a plan to eat something every half hour to keep his strength up. This certainly made sense, but I could not manage it as I could not let go of my paddle. The adrenalin would keep me going! He also had his special pee bottle ready in case of emergencies. Again I would either have to wait or wet myself! The joys of being female.

The Wollaston Islands looked a long way ahead, low and hazy. We paddled towards a twin-peaked mountain, bearing 180 degrees. I could hardly believe that we would ever get there. The coast of Navarino Island crept into the distance; but the Wollaston Islands were not getting any closer. Albatrosses glided over the sea, and the odd skua sat large and threatening on the jubbly surface.

After two hours we had only covered five miles, and the word from *Compass Rose* was we must go faster. But now we were further from the coast the swell became larger and a tail wind was building. This filled me with horror, as we were now completely committed.

Nigel and JW stuck close to me. Nigel called up Jack on *Compass Rose* and said that he would not call on the radio again, but if he needed assistance he would raise his paddle. This sounded worrying.

The weather did not deteriorate, but the swell increased so much that sometimes the other boats disappeared for a few seconds in troughs. I kept looking ahead at Cape Ross, the closest point on the Wollaston Islands. The cliffs were getting larger, we were getting closer, but there was still plenty of time for something to go wrong.

My right knee was stiff but I could not move it because the bilge pump was in the way. My heels were also tender, as if I had blisters – the last thing I expected from kayaking, but they were continually rubbing on my boots and often wet, so the skin was soft, despite the Ko-cho-line that Dad and I swear by, the red grease used for the treatment of leather which we put on our feet every morning. My hands were freezing, but no more blisters, and my wrists were fine.

When *Compass Rose* came close for Jack to film from the bow I tensed up, throwing my kayak this way and that, and wondered if I could be sucked in under her propeller. The wind continued to change strength, but we were on the final leg now. I was tired, but by no means exhausted and the team was jubilant as a couple of dolphins leapt clear of the water, making a blowing noise, their sleek shiny bodies moving so easily through the waves that tossed us wherever they pleased.

Nigel asked if everyone was all right to go on beyond Cape Ross to the radio station, where there was a sheltered landing beach. All I could see on the seaward side was cliffs. As we approached the coast the swell seemed to get larger and all I could think about was having a pee. The rushing water made it worse! JW and Nigel whizzed past me, doing terrific surfing, but I just played it safe, not wanting to go in now after the five hours of surviving! At last, after five and a half hours, we reached the sheltered waters of the bay on the other side of Cape Ross. Here the kelp formed a thick carpet almost impenetrable by our paddles. Some strands were as thick as my wrist.

Compass Rose called us to say that the three radio operators were looking forward to the first new faces they would have encountered for forty-five days! I could see two men in black and a husky-type dog down on the beach. I waved to them with sheer joy. We had survived. Spared by natural forces once more.

Levering my stiff body out of my cockpit on to the shore, I was now quite desperate to go to the loo and hobbled off across slippery kelp-covered slabs to find a secluded spot. Struggling with stiff knee, blistered heels, numb hands and various layers of waterproofs, spray decks and thermals, I made it! The wild-eyed husky glared at me, but I was too elated to even think that it might attack.

As I wobbled stiffly back to the water's edge, Dad was introducing himself to the two bemused radio operators as the oldest man ever to paddle across Bahia Nassau. It took us a long time to get all the kayaks up on to the safety of a grassy bank, as instead of the usual two to lift a single, it now took four – a mark of how much our morning rigours had taken out of us, and it was only 10.30 a.m.

The whole yacht team came ashore once *Compass Rose* was moored, full of cheer and congratulations. Conrado embraced us all with huge bear hugs and bristly kisses. He was very emotional about our achievement. I asked Eduardo if there was any chance of us going to the radio operators' hut for a cup of tea before we got ourselves sorted out. I told him to tell them that la señorita was very tired. I might as well make use of being the only weedy female in this chauvinistic country! It worked.

The radio station proved to be an airtight module of twenty-first-century technology on a lonely island near the end of the earth, with TV, videos, showers, a generator which ran all the time to power the large bank of radios, electric lights and overpowering heat. We could hardly believe it.

From the window of the radio control room, we could see the route we had come. Now the wind was howling, the sea violent and a mass of white. Shivers ran down my spine, behind the safe double-glazed windows. How lucky we had been.

The radio operators provided warm showers, they dried our clothes, and plied us with coffee and freshly baked buns. While we sampled their few violent English-language videos, they cooked frankfurters and fried fresh potatoes, and offered us a bright pink sugary drink they loved which tasted of cherry-flavoured boiled sweets.

We stayed two days, until the weather calmed down, sleeping in the spare bunks and on the floor. We cooked dehydrated food for them; it was odd what different tastes they had to us, hating Marmite, but loving apple flakes and custard! They were low on supplies, so we gave them some of our food in return for letting us stay. The Chilean flag above the station was becoming shredded by the battering wind. This was no time to be on the water. Once all the videos had been watched, there was not much for our keen team to do. We could not walk on the island, as Eduardo and the radio operators said there were mines, and anyway the wind was so strong we could hardly stand up outside. But we were now a good team and got on well together, almost unheard of in these situations.

I slept for half of the next day, 18 January, Mum's birthday, and thought of her at home in a similar situation to us, holed up from the fierce weather. The following night, Igor disrupted the whole southern Chile communications network by getting the three radio operators drunk until midnight, then having to sleep off their hangovers until mid-morning! The generator went down, and no one was on duty! They crawled around looking terrible the next morning: Igor was fine.

The forecasts from every available source were not good, and Nigel was getting impatient. It was decided that as soon as the mended flag hung limp and the wind began to blow from the north-west, we must leave, making the most of the next available window in the weather once more. So we said our farewells to the kind and hungover radio operators and their scavenging dogs and headed out into the kelp.

Although the wind had gone round, and we should be in the lee of the land, it was very gusty, paddles buffeted. But Nigel and Aled came into their own as we skirted bays and crossed to downwind points at the right times, making the most of the wind and sea. These were the worst conditions for me. I was forever looking round so that I could see the gusts coming. The water would become dark and ruffled with a mist of white sea spray blowing above the surface, then it hit you. The gusts were so strong, that even by bracing, leaning on your paddle with blade flat on the water's surface, we sped along as fast as if we had been paddling. Sometimes I felt myself tensing up, overcome with fear, looking around for Dad and checking that Nigel was still near me. I don't think Nigel thought I was going to go in, but I had a few wobbles! Aled stayed close to Dad, JW liked to be quite separate and the doubles were having a great time, stable and powering down the waves. We passed huge colonies of terns. They are the most beautiful birds, so petite, graceful and delicate.

We made a dramatic and speedy crossing of Bahia Alsina, where the wind blew relentlessly, Nigel shouting to me to aim for various points, then just to aim for the shore to find shelter! We were all exhilarated by the exciting weather, but conscious that if something went wrong, we would be blown out to sea fast, with little chance of making it back to land in a weakened state.

With the relief of getting to the headland at the southern side of Bahia Alsina, we sped in between a rock and the cliffs. I followed Nigel closely, knowing that he would have chosen the timing correctly, but Dad followed shortly after me and the timing was slightly out. I think he was so relieved at having made it safely across the bay, that he was now not really thinking. The swell came in and swept him backwards towards the rocks, where he disappeared behind a wall of surf, only his paddle visible. He always acted strangely in these situations. Most people would paddle furiously in a panic and possibly get free by chance or capsize, but Dad would freeze, not paddling at all, as if waiting to see what the sea would do to him! I saw a paddle in the air, and as the wave sunk down again, Dad was sucked in sideways towards the steep rock-face, but somehow he managed to stay upright and pushed off with his paddle. We all shouted, "Paddle, paddle," desperately, but he could not hear for breaking waves. Eventually he did paddle slowly clear of the rocks. He laughed weakly, so did we with relief!

We picked our way through some narrow channels between tall stacks of dark rock, the sea rising and falling gently with the swell, and stopped for a late lunch in a rocky bay bordered by cliffs, all quite cold but excited by the wind.

Pressing on into the much larger Bahia Hately, the wind became stronger, and more gusty. Now we paddled into it. The kelp was thick, so progress slow. At least it was easier to see the gusts coming, head down and paddling slowly but strongly, often not going forward more than a few inches! We stayed close to the shore, but the wind was funnelled along the cliffs. On the other side of the bay, great white plumes of spray whirled high into the air and at great speed along the surface.

Above the noise of the wind tearing at our ears, a haunting, almost human crying sound could be heard. Were there survivors from a shipwreck stranded in one of these dark caves? What could be making such a wailing noise? Drawn towards the sound, we found a large cave, its rocky floor crowded with sea lions. Two large bulls, great rolls of blubber around their thick necks, lunged at us as we ventured in closer, but did not enter the water. The cave echoed with the different pitches of their cries as they became more frenzied. The fishy smell was overpowering. Boycie filmed from the front of his double kayak, urging Chris to paddle closer, closer, as the rest of us back-paddled out into the light where two black scavenger birds screamed for the next dead pup or scraps of fish, and a small otter popped its head up amongst the kelp, and climbed on to a seaweed-covered rock for a better look at us before slithering back into the water in disbelief. It reminded me of the otters at Ardmore who stitch the water so playfully in the winter, searching for food.

With the strong wind and sea spray most of us used our poggies, waterproof mittens that fit over the paddle shaft and Velcro tight around it, leaving hands free to slip in and out. I was caught unawares by one particularly strong gust, which ripped the paddle from my hands. With no paddle it is very difficult to balance the kayak and stop it from turning over. Everything went into slow motion, Chris and Boycie were ten feet or so away and slightly ahead. As the wind tipped me almost on my side I could see their horrified expressions! The gust dropped slightly, and I managed to get my boat flat on the water again, as Nigel's words of advice came alive in my head again. "There's no use in having a paddle park, if you don't have the confidence and ability to pull your paddle back to you with it." So I grasped the piece of cord and pulled, reaching out for my paddle, now caught in some kelp under my boat. Miraculously, I managed to grasp the shaft and began to paddle slowly forward.

My heart was pounding, I had been very lucky and surely I would not be as lucky a second time. I could not believe that I had not capsized, and chattered on to Dad, reliving every moment! We were all laughing with relief.

It was getting quite late now, and we found a bay in which to camp right on the edge of the beach, as the dense bushes inland were almost impenetrable. Then we wrestled with the stove to cook supper in the gusty wind. We had only covered a short distance, but it had been an exciting ten miles.

18

Dolphins

I was grumpy when I woke, as it was getting light. Putting on damp clothes did nothing to improve my mood. We were slow to pack up, and Dad was getting at me to hurry up, so I handed him a hot saucepan! He was not impressed.

We were on the water by 5.30 a.m. I was still in a bad mood, but Conrado had radioed that the weather forecast was promising and the morning indeed looked good, with a huge clear horizon and a vast area of unthreatening sky out to the north-east. The southern shore of Bahia Hatley reminded me of the west coast of Scotland. We could so easily have been paddling into Glen Dhu, down by Kylesku, the steep browny hillside broken up by large outcrops of rock.

We paddled directly across Bahia Hately, the sea flat and silky, flecked with pale blues and greys of the sky. Nigel suggested we might get to Cape Horn today, jokingly, I thought, and I agreed, assuming this would not be the case.

Once we crossed the bay, we paddled close to the headland, where Savage ducks and shags took off with alarm as we passed, and a strong fishy smell lingered in the still air. Dark fins began to appear well off shore. What were they? Would they be friendly or would they attack us? We paddled towards them all the same. One of the highlights of the trip for me was paddling amongst these dolphins. A school had been attracted by *Compass Rose*, and swam with her bow wave. Then they found us, too. They moved at great speed, leaping close to each other clear of the water. Sometimes we could see them swim under our kayaks to re-emerge on the other side. We probably travelled at double our normal paddling speed to try and keep up. I was so thrilled by being among these intelligent wild creatures, I did not take in any of Bahia Scourfield, which came next, and when we reached

Freycinet Island, the dolphins, sadly, left us, maybe because of the kelp.

Eduardo went crazy as we stopped for a rest by an unused navy hut, and started to walk up to investigate it. He got Conrado to motor in close with *Compass Rose* and shouted that we should not land as this was a restricted area. JW loved this and made sure that he had got a few photographs before we left, as well as a handful of spent bullets, which most of the chaps collected!

Leaving the forbidden hut, so as not to upset Eduardo too much, we paddled on south between Wollaston and Freycinet Islands, where the tide ran strongly. There was an oily, fishy smell on the air, which reminded Dad of whale's breath but we did not see one. We paddled on towards the southern end of Herschel Island, through Bahia Arquistade. Maybe we really would reach Cape Horn today. The weather was still good, not flat calm as it had been earlier, but good for covering the distance.

A couple of large brown Sooty albatrosses with long lumpy beaks sat still on the water as we paddled closer and closer to them, flapping their wings pathetically at the last minute to lift their heavy bodies clear of possible danger.

We paddled quite separately, filled with thoughts of Cape Horn. What would Cape Horn Island look like? We had all seen postcards and photographs of it, and knew what shape it was from the chart, but how would it appear to us the first time we saw it? Was its weather going to show us any mercy, or would we end our days in the tempestuous waters around its fortress-like coast?

As we entered Paso Mar del Sur, we could hear the sound of light-aircraft engines. First one, then a second tiny grey dot in the sky became larger, heading towards us. These must have been the small planes that it is possible to charter to fly down and around Cape Horn, if you are wealthy enough and do not want to go on the water! They spotted us, and swooped down circling us twice to get a better look. I waved my paddle and felt proud that I was down here, not up there!

We stopped for lunch at the old naval hut on the south-eastern corner of Herschel Island. It was surrounded by great coils of terrible-looking wire, worse than barbed wire, it had small razor blades in it. A couple of decomposing penguins lay on the path up to the hut, which did not look too bad from the outside, but inside was grim, everything coated in a damp, greasy dust, and the place pretty well wrecked. Once it must have been a well-looked-after and well-equipped military building, but now it was left to ruin. Frank Goodman and his team stayed here on 20 and 21 December 1977, before rounding Cape Horn on 22 December; fourteen years later, little can have changed down here, except the state of the hut.

We ate our lunch in the main room, everyone in high spirits as we were so close to our goal. The weather looked fine, we had already covered twenty miles, it was still only midday, and none of us felt tired. Should we, like Frank Goodman, go for the circumnavigation now from here? Or should we make for the only landing beach on Cape Horn Island and wait until the weather was suitable? Would it be too much of a risk to set off now, halfway through the day, when we were not fresh? What if the weather changed? We could be left to face difficult if not impossible conditions when tired with darkness coming on. We also had to think about timing for our television and newspaper commitments. To get good film of the notorious cliffs of Cape Horn the helicopter needed to come and the *Castor* had to get into position in the middle of Bahia Nassau, which would all take at least seven hours. So our decision was made for us.

The weather was already changing, as we emerged into the open water for the four-mile crossing to Cape Horn. Dad paddled with Aled and *Rockwater 7*, while I stuck close to Nigel and JW. The sun had gone, everything became dark. Looking behind, rain was coming, the sea was menacing again. Cape Horn Island became dark purple, the clouds above it heavy and black, I could see the jagged peak of Cape Horn on the other side. The wind blew up, white horses appeared on the sea, then the rain came, chilling our hands but calming the wind.

I felt very much in awe of the surroundings, Deceit Island which we passed on our left was jagged cliff. There was no mercy there. Ahead were more inhospitable cliffs and just one beach for which we were aiming, below a radio station and lighthouse. We were but tiny fragments on the great ocean, hoping we were in control, but knowing that in reality the sea and wind could do with us what they chose.

We landed safely and tied our kayaks to the smart wooden handrail of the steps that led to the buildings at the top of the cliff. A sign read "Welcome to Penguin City" and there was a white monument to the Cape Horners with a large Chilean flag flying high above. Penguin City consisted of a radio hut, generator shed, church and lighthouse.

Leaving our kit and wellies outside by a heavily pregnant dog, we went into the mustard-coloured hardboard-lined radio hut. This was not like Cape Ross, these three radio operators had frequent visits from passing yachts and other boats, but not many kayakists! They showed us the flags of the nations along the top of one wall, the portraits of famous Chilean naval captains and various mementoes left by travellers. Coffee and buns were produced as we discussed their relief map of Cape Horn Island.

The lieutenant in charge of the two younger operators was small with bright friendly dark eyes, thick black hair, black moustache and round cheeks, the only lines on his face were from smiling. He gallantly gave me a bucket of hot water to wash myself and my clothes, and offered me the bathroom first. By the time I emerged, a south-westerly gale was blowing, and from the window that looked back across the straits of Herschel and Deceit Islands the sea hundreds of feet below was streaked with white and very rough. We had had another narrow escape.

After supper and the obligatory violent American video, we turned in. I slept on the top of the only spare bunk, with Dad underneath and everyone else on the floor.

The wind was still howling next morning and Nigel had already decided that today was out. After breakfast we planned to climb to the top of Cape Horn. But first I tried to treat the chief radio operator's toothache with oil of cloves from my first-aid kit, as he could not get to a dentist for three weeks.

Boycie, Nigel, Hoppy, JW and I got ready to walk to the top of Cape Horn in our wellies, thermals and waterproofs. Igor and Eduardo were going to come part of the way, Eduardo to show us a path that led round the hill to the large bay on the southern side of the island and up the edge of the cliff to the top. We passed a wired-in minefield, and strode off along the narrow path, which soon petered out, leaving us struggling through waist-deep southern beech, now growing dense and horizontal to the ground. It was just like running through the heather, gathering the sheep from Ardmore Point during the summer for shearing, when I am shepherd and sheepdog. Large cushions of thick, strong, pale-green star-shaped moss were the only stable footholds. Once we had struggled down to the bay, we came across a penguin rookery. Some had their burrows quite a way from the water, waddling backwards and forwards over rounded rocks, up steep slippery mud banks, then through tunnels in the undergrowth to their muddy homes. Most of the young seemed fairly grown up, with just the remnants of baby feathers. Some hissed at us when we got too close, necks bent forwards and heads on one side, in the most fierce pose a penguin can produce. Two large eagle-like birds sat high on jagged rocks at the end of the beach, waiting for their lunch, while a pair of ashy-headed geese grazed one of the few small patches of grass above.

Like the penguins, we hopped from smooth rock to rock, and now the wind had died away and the sun was hot, we peeled our extra layers down round our waists. There was great communication between Nigel and Dad on the hand-held VHF radio, now the weather had changed for the better, about the best time to paddle to the top end of the island where we could make an interim camp. All this needed planning: the forecast was good for the next day, the helicopter should be put on alert, so that it could arrive at Cape Horn early the next morning, and we could be in position off the cliffs for the filming. As if getting round Cape Horn was not enough of a challenge without accommodating a television schedule.

At the end of the beach, we began our ascent, keeping to the edge of the cliff where there was little undergrowth. The heat was intense and we were all thirsty. A little way below the summit, we came across a hidden loch. It was dark and calm with a family of ducks swimming serenely around. Only a short distance and a huge drop to its left lay the most terrifying and turbulent seas in the world, but the loch had an uncanny stillness about it.

Once on the top of the fearsome cliffs, we searched in vain for the message Frank Goodman had left in a bottle, but we did find a piece of wood carved to commemorate a French and Chilean kayak expedition and a message in Spanish wrapped up in plastic, which none of us could read. We left our own message in a bottle, took lots of photographs with the self-timer of the five of us with my Union Jack, and peered along the coast for any possible emergency landing points. The northern end of the island, with its stacks, was the most dramatic, with Wollaston and Navarino Islands beyond, looking beautiful on a good day. As we descended we all knew that the next time we saw those cliffs close to would be from sea level.

We decided to depart at 4 a.m., and discussion about the helicopter and the weather went on all through supper. *Compass Rose* would anchor in the bay, close to the landing beach, Richard and Jack would sleep ashore to film us leaving in the dark, then wait for the helicopter.

The hut was hot with last-minute clothes-drying, and noisy with violent television and fervent discussion. I went outside to be alone and visit the church. The evening sky was filled with mares' tails. High winds – had the right decision been made? I nipped back into the hut to warn Nigel and Dad. Leaving the weathermen to further discussion I went and stood silently in the most southerly church in the world. Painted in red on rough white planks to the right of the double door were the words "*Capilla Naval Stella-Maris Cabo De Hornos Chile*". Above the door was a thin white cross. Up three steps and through the brown doors that stuck on the uneven linoleum, and one was look-ing at two rows of rough benches facing an altar supported by two tree trunks, and covered in a lace cloth. On it were a pair of vases of plastic flowers, three candlesticks and a cross. Behind, on the rough wooden wall, hung a larger cross of dark polished wood. The three windows on each side of the church let in plenty of light. Moss grew around the edges of the small panes of uneven-quality glass. They reminded me of old Highland windows. Each one held a fantastic view. The grey linoleum was wet from the rain that had driven through the bark-covered planks of the windward wall. In one corner stood the Virgin Carmen, the patron saint of Chile, in another a sailor's dress jacket with seven brass buttons down the front and three on the cuffs, displayed in a case.

I stood still, looking at the altar, then out of the window that framed Cape Horn. I could see the route we took to climb to the top, the sky lit up with varying shades of orange behind the Cape, and no land beyond until Antarctica.

In my diary, before I went to sleep, I wrote, "Standing alone in the small church, I asked God to do with us what he would and to guide us." If we were meant to succeed we would. Beyond all our judgement and careful planning, I felt that fate held us, as it had done in Peru six years earlier, when we found Elizabeth.

19

Pitch and Toss

I woke at 2.30 a.m. hot and anxious, rather like waking up on the day of exams. Although I was looking forward to the paddle, I did feel extremely nervous, but managed to doze again until my alarm went at 3 a.m. Coffee and a couple of oatcakes with Marmite made a quick breakfast. In the pitch dark outside, everyone rushed around collecting their kit for the great day. There was not much chat. Dad and I walked down the steps to our boats in silence. My heart thumped as I packed away my sleeping-bag, the taste of rubber in my mouth as I held the torch between my teeth.

Jack was dashing around with his camera, filming and blinding us as we got our boats on the water. Dad was away first into the darkness, only the reflective strip on the back of his buoyancy aid picking up flickers of torch light.

I climbed into my boat, pulling the back rest up behind me, and checking my footrests were secure and had not moved. Richard wished me good luck, as I tried to put the twin seals of my spray deck on quickly with shaking hands. I felt so nervous, but knew that once I was on the water I would calm down. Jack's spotlight shone on me as I slid down the rocks into the water.

The moon hung pale and large in the dark sky above, its light catching the odd surface ripple, as we paddled north with the tide against us most of the way. Dawn was already taking the place of night and the inhospitable coastline of Cape Horn Island looked even more sinister in the half-light.

We paddled quite separate, hardly uttering a word. Dad chewed gum furiously, in deep concentration. I wondered what this trip would mean to the others in the future. After two years of planning and so many hours of training it would soon be over. If we succeeded, we would be jubilant, but afterwards there would be a gap to fill. For most of us, our energies would need to turn to some other struggle. I know it is addictive.

At the north-western corner of the island we met the Southern Ocean swell. I paddled some distance in front of Dad, but JW was with him, so I felt he was safer than with me. The swell was long and deep, much larger than we had paddled on before, but being so long, it was slow, and easy to handle. It was just the changing elevation that was slightly alarming, like the difference between looking out on the world from the roof of a house one minute and from its garden the next.

I stopped paddling when I caught up with Nigel, and waited for Dad and JW. The next bit did not look so easy. Dad gave me a few sharp words for not waiting for him, and we continued. He was chewing his gum even harder. I did not feel too bad, but knew there could be some hairy moments ahead. We now had to turn south past cliffs with towering stacks and huge rocks off shore. The sea looked confused, with the large swell coming in, hitting the cliffs and bouncing back against other swells marching in; this is called clapotis, pointy waves that lift you up, usually with not much water on either side, then suddenly fall away and drop you. The waves bouncing back off the cliff were often breaking waves by the time they reached us. Now paddling broadside to all of this, we had to stay relaxed and aware, to survive the choppy sea.

Compass Rose was well off shore now. I watched her heaving around in the swell, sometimes seeing her hull, sometimes only part of her mast. To our right was a small island-sized rock, the surf rushing up and down its jagged sides like claws, growling, a mass of white. JW and I paddled close together, if I went over now, would I really have the presence of mind to roll up again? This would not be the place to come out of the kayak. JW and I chatted, interspersed by my squawks every time I saw a challenging wave hurtle towards me! I knew I must stay relaxed. Ahead, I could see two figures, one looking straight in front, sitting stiffly in his boat – Dad; the other relaxed, often turning to encourage – Nigel.

I had a few quite serious wobbles, but managed to correct myself, the worst being caused by a wave I saw coming, and braced into as it broke over my head. Somehow I emerged the right way up and continued paddling, blinking the salt out of my eyes, and grinning with sheer joy at having survived.

What surprised me when I first started sea kayaking, was the continual changing state of the sea. On a larger boat, or from the land, to most of us the sea looks the same. It is either rough, calm or in between, but when you are sitting low in the water in a kayak, you notice that it is continually changing with tide, currents, wind and swell, and close to the shore, the characteristics of the coastline and depth of water also have an effect. Learning to read the sea is an important part of making paddling as easy and safe as it can be, which on a long and potentially dangerous trip will be the difference not only between exhaustion and feeling pleasantly tired, but possible total disaster and success.

Once we had got past the tricky north-western corner of the island, we had a slightly easier paddle across a wide open bay well inland towards the next headland which had several offshore rocks. Should we go round the outside or through the gap between the shore and first rock? I was all for going round the outside, but Nigel said it was rougher out there and as long as our timing through the gap was right it would be fine. I had watched some large rollers crash through the gap. We had to go through on one of the smaller ones, avoiding the kelp and rocks. I went first, as soon as I thought it was right and the others said go. I whizzed through, heart in mouth, pushed along by the wave and paddling like mad. In front of me I could see kelp and rocks, but as I sped towards them, the wave I was on took me clearly over the top.

Now we could see the 1400-foot cliffs of Cape Horn towering above us to our left. They looked greener than the pictures I had seen of them, but just as terrifying. Just looking up made you dizzy, and you could not forget the miles and miles of open sea, which at any minute might become an impossible place for us fragile beings to survive, nor the desperate dramas played out here over the centuries.

As we paddled right under the cliffs, the sun shone, and everyone grinned. The weather had held, we had almost made it. Then the helicopter swooped in to film us and we tried to remember not to look up at it. Even in such a moment of triumph, a shiver ran down my spine at the sound of the rotors, which I always feel is as sinister as it is deafening. Now we were paddling across the bay we had walked round the day before, and we knew we were going to make it.

The sun was brilliant, Nigel, JW and I took photographs of each other. Penguins swam near to us as we approached the south-easterly point and *Compass Rose* came closer to congratulate us.

After nearly six hours covering the twelve-mile circumnavigation, the bow of my trusty 18-foot yellow and white fibreglass kayak crunched up on to the same grey pebbled beach last seen in the dark at 4 a.m.

Against most of the odds, and other people's opinions, our nine-strong team had completed the two-hundred-mile trip in ten days of paddling in the most treacherous sea area of the world, and I had become the first female to kayak right round Cape Horn Island.